ADVANCE PRAISE

As the CEO of a technology company I've been the "cause" of some "unwanted and unplanned" career transitions. I've been involved at the beginning and the end of many career transition journeys—at times I've delivered the shock of termination, and other times, I've shared in the delight and relief that the sought-after job offer brings. However, despite this involvement at both ends of the career transition process, I hadn't given much thought to the part in between—the agonizing, frightening, demanding and uncertain part, and the part faced, not just by the individual but by their entire family.

Until, that is, I read this book!

I met George during his first unplanned career transition. I was one of the executives he boldly reached out to and introduced himself. His tenacity and humility resulted in "coffee" meetings and ultimately my considering him for a position within my organization.

In this book, George captures the gamut of emotions he faced during his enforced career transitions, but he doesn't stop there. He goes on to articulate his learned "best practices" and translates them into concise, practical, relevant, clear and relatively easy-to-apply tips and strategies. These tips and strategies are of value, not only to those experiencing "unwanted" career transition but also to those wishing to understand, support and help those going through a transition.

George calls upon his military background, his years of leadership, his humility, his faith, and his organizational skills to craft the set of practical, organized tips and strategies that you are about to read. The beauty of what George offers is you can easily apply/implement only those tips and strategies *that will work best for you.*

George Murray is a humble, committed and highly credible executive who has experienced the highs and lows of unwanted career transitions. He has learned from them and is now "giving back" by sharing his learning with you, the reader.

By investing your time reading this book and deploying the tips and strategies that you feel are right for you, you will significantly condense the duration of your own transition or be better equipped to understand and support those you love or care about as they navigate their own unwanted career transition.

—**Dr. Alan D. W. McLenaghan**,
   CEO, Saint-Gobain – SageGlass

• • •

When you first lose your job, you have no idea where to turn, who to ask for advice, or what to do first, second and so on. Neither did George, but he figured it out by asking questions and listening to all kinds of people's advice. Out of that came "Hired!" a real hands-on guide to cutting down the time of your career search—and reducing your stress and anxiety.

—**George Rye**
   Owner/CEO of R&R Business Development Company

• • •

Spectacular! I've spent 22 years in the recruiting and consulting industries. Hands-down, this is the best and most important book written by someone who has overcome a hard and painful job loss. Career transition is hard! It is lonely. George's book is the breath of fresh air and the rock-solid advice you desperately need.

While everyone else is barking about resumes, networking, and interviewing, George teaches you how to break through the biggest barriers to success (most of which are living in your head). He's refreshingly open and honest about his own internal battles and job search mistakes. Then, with a consistent beat of inspiration, he tells you how to avoid them in your search.

He nailed it! Every single piece of advice was spot-on.

—**Catherine Byers Breet**
Chief Stripe Changer | ARBEZ www.arbez.com
catherine@arbez.com | linkedin.com/in/catherinebyersbreet

• • •

George's book addresses so much more than the job transition—including getting your finances in order, teaching family members about resilience, and networking after the job search. I see this as a great reference book during different times of your life and career.

—**Jenny Jefferds**
Sales Director and New Business Development at Solutia

• • •

Through his learnings during his own career transitions, George delivers the best step-by-step guide to build your professional and personal network and walks you through your journey to land your next executive role.

—Steve Yakesh
  President, Direct Hire & Executive Search

HIRED

CUT YOUR CAREER SEARCH TIME IN HALF

KIRK HOUSE PUBLISHERS

HIRED

CUT YOUR CAREER SEARCH TIME IN HALF

GEORGE C. MURRAY

Copyright © 2020 George C. Murray

All rights reserved. This book or any portion thereof may not be reproduced or used in any manner whatsoever without the express written permission of the publisher except for the use of brief quotations in a book review.

Printed by Kirk House Publishers, in the United States of America.

First printing, October 2020

ISBN: 978-1-952976-05-6
LOC: 2020917761

Cover Design: Derek A. Friday
Interior Design: Ann Aubitz

Kirk House Publishers
1250 East 115th Street
Burnsville, MN 55337
Kirkhousepublishers.com

FOREWORD

There's only one letter differentiating "Hired" from "Fired;" both change your life. I see it every day in my work as an executive recruiter.

With great clarity, angst and personal anecdotes, George shares his story: twice in 20 months he lost his position as a result of his employers' financial issues. Twice he had to transition.

Like most in his situation, George had no training in career transition. His first took 13 months, the second, six.

Initially, George had more questions than answers about networking (when, where, who, how many), and at times questioned the value of the time and money invested. He considered how he could best market himself to those with whom he networked and interviewed. He reminds us often that we have to leave people with the "WOW!" factor—and make ourselves "memorable."

If you are in career transition, George's insights are invaluable. He provides easy-to-implement steps for much of what he learned the hard way. Tools such as his "Day in the Life," "90-Day Plan," "Executive Bio," "10-10-10," and especially the "Value Proposition" will give you a jumpstart on your own transition (Examples shown of each).

—**David Lyman**
  Lyman Executive Search
  dlyman@lymanexecutivesearch.com

DEDICATION

This book is dedicated to anyone who has or is struggling with the process of finding a new position, and is dealing with being unemployed. This book is also dedicated to those who love and live with that person—those who need to be kind, thoughtful, helpful—and above all patient.

TABLE OF CONTENTS

Acknowledgment   15

Introduction   19

1. Shock and Awe: Planning for the Next Rung to Grab Onto   21

2. The Much-Needed Tools for Success   39

3. Be the Boss of YOU: Create Your Routine, Your "Day in the Life"—and Live It   59

4. Be Prepared: Every Networking Opportunity Counts   77

5. Many "How-To's" to Land Your Next Position   99

6. Your "Job," While Looking for a Job   115

7. Roadmap to a Successful Transition   125

About the Author   131

ACKNOWLEDGMENT

I am truly thankful to all those whom I met and who helped me through both transitions—those who have taken some of your valuable time to meet with me, and helped me move forward to #Getbetter. Your help was unmeasurable. A transition can be demoralizing, demotivating, and downright frightening. You made the whole transition process bearable for me. A lot of you lifted me up during these difficult times. I will not name everyone for fear I'd omit someone. I simply want to thank each and every one of you from the bottom of my heart.

I started #GetBetter and #StartToday early in my first career transition in 2016. As I looked in the mirror those initial days of my first job transition, I was frustrated, etc. I recall coming up with *"Each day I can #GetBetter than who I was yesterday, not get better than someone else but better than me yesterday; and I can #StartToday."* The only true competition you have in this world is who you are—and when you find out who you want to be—plan, and be relentless to that newer version of yourself that you want to be.

I couldn't have done this without the support of my wife, Kerry—and her diligence in saving money. Through our years together, she saved and scrimped and managed our money smartly to make sure we would never be lacking, but at the same time, we'd never end up in the poor house either. After 26 years and counting she has continued to amaze me, support me, and inspire me to work hard and provide the best life for our family.

Thank you to my editor, Connie Anderson, Words & Deeds, Inc., who helped me communicate clearly the process that this book articulates. I want to help all those questioning "what's next" after they hear the worlds: "Laid off, decided to go in a different direction," or "We have had to make adjustments in our cost, etc." Connie quickly realized that I wanted feedback without any sugar coating to ensure that my message came across clearly as did my intent to outline all aspects to be considered in job transition.

To my cover designer, Derek Friday, who I found by luck in the vastness of cover designers. He clearly listened to the message I was trying to convey to those in career transition and was very flexible, responsive, and hit the mark with the cover's impact.

Kathleen Crandall, Personal Brand Expert, Professional Transition & Job Search Coach, Small Business Branding, Workshops, Keynote Speaker, and Message Development—in my first transition she was extremely available with her time and skill in "Branding." I had not heard the word "Personal Branding" up till then, and she was able to clearly pull my brand out of me. A positive light during my early stage of career transition.

Anne Pryor helped skyrocket my exposure on LinkedIn and took the brand I came to understand and articulate to the world on the LinkedIn platform. Anne was always extremely flexible with her time and willing to help me during my troubled times.

My Personal Board of Advisors: Lenny Newman, Lisa Fraga, Alan McClellan, Ryan Carlson, Chris Kobold, Jenny Jefferds, and Greg Rye. You have always been there for me through both good and not-so-good times, listened, motivated, inspired, guided, and challenged me. Thank you to my financial advisors, Patti and Louis Wendling of Wendling Financial Group.

Thank you to Ann Aubitz and the team at Kirk House Publishers for their confidence in publishing my book.

INTRODUCTION

Writing this book covers 19 months of my time, as well as two career transitions, and provides you with all the necessary tools and pointers to make your time in transition shorter and more rewarding. I think I drank enough coffee to fill a small Minnesota Lake while writing it.

You're never quite prepared for your first transition, or any subsequent one for that matter. This book will take you through my personal coping process and show you how to learn the process on the fly (real-time). I wish a book had existed when I first lost my job that could have specifically outlined the coping strategies that I needed to discover and master over a 19-month period.

CHAPTER 1
Shock and Awe—Planning for the Next Rung to Grab Onto

This book was written with the intent to help a professional like yourself to speed up your career transition and to share with you the best practices that helped me quickly land my next opportunity.

I want my book to be the answer that if you've been laid off/fired/released etc. on a Friday or a Monday—you can read this book in two days and eliminate six months of trying to figure it out.

• • •

TIPS AND STRATEGIES:

Always work hard to maintain a positive attitude, be enthusiastic, and exude high energy because no one wants to talk to someone who isn't.

I was a 48-year-old introvert during my first transition. I found out later that 48 was the average age of most professionals when they find themselves outside for the first time, without the next rung to grab. This book gives a brief overview of what consumed the first seven months of my transition just trying to figure things out. I was fortunate enough to learn most of these tips, strategies, and tools during many hours of networking with all kinds of people willing to share their insights, knowledge, and personal experiences.

I was lucky enough to meet a lot of great people, learn from their trials and tribulations, and am now able to integrate all the information I gleaned into these "best practices." May they help you land your next opportunity much quicker than you would without this resource. Don't ever forget the learning experience from this journey—meeting and learning from all kinds of new people that you would probably never had had a chance to meet otherwise. Also, by extension, remember *what to do and what not to do*, both during your transition, and in life in general.

During my first transition of 13 months, I met with 446 people, which averaged about three per day. Thanks to the tools you will learn in this book, my second transition took only six months, during which I networked with 724 people—an average of seven people per day (not counting weekends and holidays).

When most of my network peers who are post-transition, say, "Wow, that's a lot!" you can also see from their body language and some of their responses that they are not all that convinced about the importance of networking. The alternative is sitting at home applying for jobs and hoping some Applicant Tracking System (ATS) or HR intern will select your resume out of the large inbox of mail. That is not a strategy or a plan—and you will be unemployed much longer.

• • •

TIPS AND STRATEGIES:

To look for a job while in transition is the hardest job.
There is no immediate monetary reward for all the efforts you put in. All the while you must maintain a first
great impression.

Showing up in a suit or in crisp business casuals is highly encouraged. Also, it's important to maintain a positive attitude, be enthusiastic, and exude high energy because no one wants to talk to an "Eeyore," the character in "Winnie the Pooh,"—who is generally characterized as-pessimistic, gloomy, and depressed.

I wrote this book because I found it took me over eight months in my first transition to create a successful process, one that I refer to as "Creating a Day in the Life." If I knew in the first week of my first job search what I know now, instead of being out of work for 13-plus months, I could have cut that time in half.

The good Lord must have heard me. I had a chance to apply that knowledge soon after, when, nine months later, I found myself out yet again, due to a reorganization. Thus, in three years, I was out a total of 19 months. I managed to burn through all of our very nice savings nest egg, and found myself being close to a whole new lifestyle; one I was not prepared to embrace.

Career transitions can be the most humbling experience in your life, especially after you've worked so many years to get to a certain status level, house, lifestyle, etc. It's frightening to think that in a six-month span you can get to the edge of the cliff of a real ego crash, financial failure, and a deep state of humility, just to name a few consequences.

Believe me, all this can put you in a deep, dark hole very quickly, if you let it. However, here are a few quotations that came to my mind early during that period, really kept me focused, and helped me push forward:

1. "*When you go through deep waters, I will be with you.*" – Isaiah 43:2
2. "*It's not how far you fall, but how far you bounce.*" – Zig Ziglar
3. "*Life never throws you the best pitches, so you need to learn how to hit the curve and the change-ups as well.*" – George Murray
4. Finally, a powerful sentence that a friend of mine sent me the week right after I lost my job: "*Sometimes I feel like giving up; then I remember I have a lot of annoying jerks to prove wrong.*"

You will have to find ways (actually quite a few ways) to keep your spirits up, your motivation level high, and preserve your ability to overcome all the obstacles that the transition will throw at you.

This book will outline a clear, overall plan to achieve all of the above, land a job, and during the transition period, learn more about yourself, what you want as well as what you don't want. Through networking, you will learn a lot from so many other people who you would not have otherwise met who been able to help. It will pay to keep your ears and eyes open during the networking process. Job opportunities will be talked about in hallways, coffee lines, and at church, just to give a few examples. I conditioned my mind to believe that at any given time of the day at least two people out there were talking about an opportunity that would be a great fit for me—and it was my responsibility to locate at least one of these persons. The only way to actually do so *is to network.*

Gratitude:

I feel very blessed that many amazing people gave me anywhere from 20 minutes to many hours of their time to share insights and provide introductions. This gave me the necessary traction to get to my final destination: a new position.

Finding gratitude during a career transition—a most difficult time in your life, you can go down two paths: 1) pity, or 2) a having a sense of gratitude for the things you have, not what you don't have.

Each morning and each night be grateful for things you have, and don't complain about the things you don't have. There are people right now who would switch places with you in a heartbeat. Someone is always far worse off than you.

• • •

TIPS AND STRATEGIES:

You might find that your life will change for the better. Mine did, once I focused on what I had rather than what I didn't have.

Even after landing a new position, each morning, as a part of my daily routine, I would still give thanks to God: "Thank you Lord for another day, thank you for my life, thank you for my family, thank you for what you have provided for me. God, I am nothing without you; I trust you to strengthen me in my weaknesses." Then I would proceed to ask Him for help like this: "Please help Jenny's Mom, Greg's Dad, and Jim's battle with cancer. May all those in a career transition; may they find new opportunities, especially those who have been out of a job for more than three months."

It certainly can be scary if you don't have a plan, you don't hustle, you don't do this, you don't do that, you don't do whatever is necessary to land a new position. But when you have faith, have a plan, have the ability to adjust your plan as is necessary 90 percent of the time, and have the "I CAN" mindset—YOU WILL be more *successful and land a new job faster.*

Mental Preparation

Before you start this journey, you need to get your mental path straight. This means that if you have been recently laid off, fired, or you left, you will first need to mentally come to terms with that upheaval. If not, it could significantly impact many factors, like your brand (more on that later), the way others look at you, and how long you will be in transition.

More about this in the "Getting Prepared" section, but I cannot stress enough the importance of taking time—two days, two weeks, two months—whatever it takes for you to get emotionally over your trauma and rationalize why you are without a job today. It is a learning experience, so learn. I have seen too many people, including myself during my first career transition, trying to move on without ever dealing with this—the first part of a successful career transition.

I feel more like a psychologist right now rather than a writer, when I say that, but it is not too far from the truth. As I write these lines, it's been over a year since I landed my new position, but I continue to meet professionals and executives in transition, and I see a high percentage of these people are skipping this critical first step.

One of my personal experiences was getting hired by a company that was in very difficult circumstances, and facing multiple cost challenges, compounded by the fact that their sales growth just could not keep pace with their costs. Being hired last on the new leadership team meant that I had very little time to reduce costs, improve processes, and adjust the company culture. My learning experience there was *to understand the timeline you have versus the timeline you think you have.* We were able to do many great things in a short time: improve customer deliveries, optimize processes, create a more ownership-focused culture, as well as develop a new generation of leaders and retain high-potential employees who were actually thinking of leaving before I came on board.

To begin this process of reviewing what happened at your last position, sit down with pen and paper either at your kitchen table, your office, or in a corner of a coffee shop. Draw three vertical lines equally spaced so you have enough room between them to make notes in each column.

Labels the three headings:
1. Why did I take this position?
2. What great things was I able to accomplish?
3. What lessons do I need to learn from problems that I didn't foresee?

"Why did I take this position?" Well, the answer to that question could be as simple as needing to work in order to pay bills. However, your motivation could have been that you wanted to get into a new industry, or you liked the description of the company culture during the interview process and from your research. This part will help you when you sit down with someone who will throw the typical first question at you: "Tell me about yourself and why you left."

"What great things was I able to accomplish?" Answering that question will put you in a very positive frame of mind, and make you proud of what you were able to accomplish at your previous job. It will help again when an interviewer asks you this question directly. It will

keep you positive even when things don't go well for you, like getting fired or laid off.

Finally, *"What lessons did I learn from problems that I didn't foresee?"* Being able to answer that question enables you to release on paper the frustration you feel from losing your previous job. It can also give you more thought clarity, help you better understand the path that you took, and the factors that eventually led to your current situation. This is the biggest part of the entire exercise. This is the most critical step for you to come to terms with your predicament and express it, on paper. You may want to throw this piece of paper away after you write it down, BUT DON'T FORGET the lesson, or you may repeat the mistake!

In the end, own it! Learn what you could have done differently, own what you didn't learn till it was too late, and what led to your current predicament. Then you can work on a path to move forward with confidence, clarity, and conviction.

Don't Take Anything Personally

From Don Miguel Ruiz, author of *The Four Agreements: A Practical Guide to Personal Freedom*—one of the most important agreements is: Don't take anything personally. This process can be frustrating, depressing, and exhausting, just to describe a few emotions. You need to find a way to rise above those things because 1) this process will take longer than expected, 2) people will not respond in the time you want, and 3) companies you interview with may not call back in your timeline. Don't take it personally. How can you do this—not take it personally? Control what you can: your attitude, your enthusiasm, and your energy. We will talk more on this throughout the book.

Stop Before You Start

I know that you are anxious to get out there and start submitting resumes, start networking, interviewing, etc. However, if you do not take the necessary time to process what just happened—you could be setting yourself up for failure. Whether you were laid off, fired, or decided to leave due to the toxic culture within your last company, you need time to process it.

I have seen people who press on without making an honest effort to answer these questions—and thus they do not have a ready, confident response to the all-important common question: "Why did you leave your last position?" It certainly does not make a great first impression when you stumble with the answer. I have seen people ramble on and on, expounding on the hostility of their previous employer or boss. The result is usually not very positive. Who wants to hire someone filled with so much negativity, even if true? I don't need to answer that; I can see on your face that speaking negatively does not sit well with others.

Each career step should be a learning experience; you may indeed have had a tough boss or a toxic work environment to deal with, but there is a learning experience in there somewhere. Find what it is and learn from it.

Then sit down again and draw a line down the middle of a blank page. On one side jot down what you liked about your previous company. Maybe the pay was good, or you truly enjoyed some of the people you worked with. Or your fancy title might have motivated you. Whatever it was, write it down. Then also write down the things that you are looking for in your next position.

On the other side of the line, jot down what you didn't like in your previous job. Perhaps it was the long hours, having to work every Saturday, or an obnoxious boss. If it was the boss, point out specifically what you didn't like about him/her. Did he scream? Did he fail to provide guidance? No mentoring/coaching, etc.? Describe the management style that you wish from your supervisors in your next position. Prepare pointed questions that will clarify and sharpen the job description of your next position to ensure that you will be making the right move.

Take a week if you need to, as long as you deeply process what happened. Talk to close friends (not your new network yet or potential employers in interviews) to process it.

In my case, at the beginning of my first transition *I was in a state of shock.* I was absolutely outraged because, all modesty aside, of the incredible improvements that I was able to make during my tenure with the company that just laid me off. But I also had to concede that the company was over-leveraged and hemorrhaging money. Looking back, from a pure business standpoint, I could rationalize why I was laid off. At that time, I was utterly frustrated and angry at having been misled. I kept that frustration in me for at least the first four months of my transition, while looking for a new career opportunity. When I look back, I am sure that my frustration invariably showed whenever I was asked the dreaded, "Why did you leave your last position" question, whether it was at an interview or a networking event. I typically rambled on and on well over 10 minutes, fumbling my way through the answer. I now know *this really hurt my chances of getting hired.*

Not until I went to a networking event and heard a career coach and outplacement professional speak about the do's and don'ts of interviewing, did it hit me. At break time I pulled him aside and tried to describe my situation to him. His response still reverberates in my mind. "Oh, you are hurting yourself," he said, after listening to me for about three minutes, while I painstakingly tried to tell him why I left my last position. He said: "You need to get past the past, learn as much as you can from it and move forward, and I give you permission." Then he told me exactly what I needed to say whenever that question came up again.

He said, "In the first 20–30 seconds, you should outline why you took the position in the first place, and in the next 30 seconds outline the good metrics that you were able to impact. Then, in 5–10 seconds, state why you left. For example: "I was impacted by a restructuring operation to reduce costs," or "I was laid off, or affected by a reduction in workforce." All of these are perfectly understandable and valid reasons to be let go, and a normal part of business life. It seemed so simple, and I finally realized that *I was taking my release as a personal humiliation.* I suddenly felt liberated, and just like that I realized I was both wasting time and impacting my brand negatively because I focused on the past and took my being laid off as a personal affront.

• • •

TIPS AND STRATEGIES:

Look at yourself in the mirror. Take a real close look. When I lost my job, I had to be brutally honest with myself for the first time in decades.

We are so busy in normal life looking at others, looking at situations, always pushing forward, and reacting. But when was the last time you honestly (both internally and externally) looked at yourself in the mirror and asked:

- "What is it that I like about me?"
- "Where am I coming up short?"
- "What is in my power to change in order to improve my life?"

When I did that, I realized that I had gained 40-plus pounds, my skin looked somewhat dull, my eyes looked tired, and my hair was probably a bit too long for my age. Our days seem to just flow along and we get up and shave, brush our teeth, etc. but when is the last time you truly looked in the mirror at yourself? If you haven't changed your look since the '80s, including your hairstyle, this may be a great time for the caterpillar to come out as a butterfly. I have networked with scores of executives and professionals who hadn't changed their haircut or made improvements in their style and clothing in 20 years—and it showed!

A true career TRANSITION requires that you do keep the positive things from the past that have helped you get to this point, and leave the rest behind. Get out and start a health program and get a new haircut. You have to feel good about yourself before others can feel good about you. Control the things that are within your control: your looks, your health, your sleep routine, your eating habits, your general outlook on life. All those things are within your control.

Get a new haircut ($100 or less, gel, hair color), lose 20 pounds, take stock of the positive things in your life that you are thankful and grateful for. I guarantee you will feel better, look better, and others will want to be around you more. With a little time, a little money, and a bit of effort, you can transform yourself into a new person, the kind of human being that you always wanted to be.

Stephen Covey says in his book that if you want small changes in your life, you need to change your attitude; if you want large changes you need to change your paradigms. I learned to be comfortable being uncomfortable. Dealing with Career Transition will definitely get you to an uncomfortable stage first.

Ditch the Entitlement Mentality—and Pick up a Bit of Humility

In both my career transitions, and by listening and helping others, I have witnessed both states of mind (Entitlement/Humility), and humility advances you more in the long run than entitlement. A transition takes work; for most of you it will be the toughest job you have had in quite some time. Not knowing how to approach your transition, not having a large network outside of your last company, etc. will be just some of the challenges you will be facing.

However, taking the humble approach will get you more support and help than coming across as a "been there, done that" type guy, or "I was a Senior Executive of XYZ company" kind of haughty person. The keyword here is "was."

This book will take you through a methodical process. If you approach it with humility, a willingness to listen and learn, your transition will be a lot easier. You will meet a lot of great people that you would not have had a chance to meet otherwise. You will learn new things about yourself and others, as well as develop an ability to self-reflect.

Being an executive or high-ranking senior professional that comes off this way is part of a concept that my good friends Anne and Lenny refer to as "TUGS": Takers-Users-Givers-Sharers.

- Takers and Users have a "me" attitude and continually take, at the expense of relationships and networks.
- Givers and Sharers are the ones that you can continue to rely on well past your transition, and your relationship with them is a two-way street.
- Being a Giver and Sharer will also put you ahead of the competition from the Takers and Users, in both the short- and long-term. Give and you will receive back in spades.

A transition is obviously a delicate stage in your life, and a certain vulnerability typically comes with it. The one thing you can't afford to tarnish is your brand, and I have seen my share of Takers and Users eventually having to pay a price for their selfish habits. The word gets out around the network, they get less and less support, and then they wonder why it is so difficult to network and land a new opportunity.

I've networked with a great number of professionals in transition who have realized that in their former job they were super busy and focused on their job, but were not really happy. Why do we pursue happiness so late in life? I can answer that because I fell into the same programmed process. It's because we pursue and chase happiness, when in effect true happiness comes from within. By contrast, the society we live in focuses on the exterior. My career transition forced me to focus for a change on my internal self, and reflect on what I could control. You can actually control your happiness if you focus on it to the same degree as you focus on a goal like your next career position. Others will notice. You will show up at each meeting, networking event, and interview with a lot more energy, enthusiasm, and positive attitude. *Let's face it, people want to be around people who are positive, high energy, and enthusiastic.* Don't be pessimistic, gloomy, or depressed—and don't be Entitled. Be Humble!

Getting Prepared

Several questions come to your mind when you find yourself in your first or a new career transition. A basic question you need to ask yourself and put a timeframe to is "How long will it take me to find another job"? Even when the economy is doing great, both professionals and executives will need a certain amount of time to find their next position. Setting a timeline of perhaps 6, 9 or 12 months, can help you deal with obstacles of both a financial and mental nature.

Some fundamental questions you should ask yourself are:

- Do I necessarily want to jump into a similar position, job, career?
- Or is this a "Day of Reckoning" for me?
- Should I make a career shift or a more radical change, and do something that I am truly passionate about?
- Should I start my own business?

A transition can be overwhelming at first, but it can also be very inspirational. You get a chance to learn about yourself. Review and question the path you have been on thus far; you can review and change accordingly. *Let it be so.*

• • •

TIPS AND STRATEGIES:

If you do not take the time to honestly reflect and come to terms with why you are at this stage in your life, your next steps will be much more difficult, and you will continue to struggle.

As said earlier, you have to take time to process what recently happened (Reduction in Workforce, laid off, etc.) Whatever it was, you first need to come to grips with the "why." You have to go through the various stages of frustration, getting rid of your mental "waste matter," and eventually accept your situation to get you past the emotional stage of distress. Get angry about why they laid you off, and cry for all the overtime, hard work, and precious years of your life that you sacrificed for the company, only to be on the other side of the fence now. However, you need to get these bad emotions out of your mindset in order to get to the next steps of your transition.

Cut that negative baggage loose and let it go. Rationalize your situation in a way that you can justify in positive terms to others. You need to crystalize that in the form of a one or two-line statement that includes the positive spin of what you learned, and how you developed and improved. The shorter the better as it's all about the past that you cannot change, and the person listening to you does not want to hear a long diatribe.

> A good example might be:
> *"I was XX at Company A for 4 years; I was part of a reduction in workforce. I enjoyed my time with Company A as I was able to do XX Project, saved the company $$, and developed good cross-departmental relationships. I am looking at your Company because I will bring X, Y, and Z to the table."*

If you take more than 20 seconds, you are rambling; you truly haven't clarified anything, and probably haven't cut that negative baggage loose yet.

Next, you must create a paragraph of introduction, describing in a nutshell who you are, what your core strengths are, and how your skills and experience can benefit the company.

A better-known term for that is "Your elevator pitch," but in my opinion that expression is already a bit passé, overused, and sounds too similar to what everyone else uses. Indeed, for a long time the standard expression has been the "60-second Elevator Pitch/Speech." But I believe it is possible, even desirable, to give a summary in 30 seconds or less of your core strengths and the reasons why you are a good candidate for the job. Your brevity will sustain your listeners' attention span and enhance your hire-ability.

I call my 30-second introduction a Value Proposition Statement. It's good to have two-to-three varieties of these statements to choose from, depending on your listener.

It's advisable to research the individual you are interviewing with, perhaps trying to tie a recent business challenge facing the company, or a personal interest of the interviewer, to your strengths so that the initial introduction is more genuine and resonates with the listener. Social media (LinkedIn, Facebook, Twitter, and so on) is replete with information on almost anyone in business.

However, always have a standard general pitch at the ready, one that gives just enough intriguing information to spark the conversation.

One of mine favorites is:

"Hello, I am George Murray, I am a Global Operations leader and US Army veteran with more than 18 years' experience with multiple P&L manufacturing operations around the globe. I have created new verticals and business transformations for Public, Private and Private Equity firms in the Automotive, Electronics Assembly, Industrial Automation and RFID industries. One of my most challenging opportunities occurred while I was on an international assignment in Thailand for three months. During a historic flood, my six factories took on 25 feet of water. Needless to say, quick action was required to salvage the situation, and we were back to normal in less than 80 days without losing and impacting a single one of our 250 customers."

Calendar

Whether it's digital, or even a manual/printed paper one, you really need to use a calendar during your transition. It is necessary to block out certain times to develop your "Day in the Life" exercise, for network events, etc. If you do not make this calendar your best friend during your career transition, before you know it, four months will have gone by, and precious little of your efforts will be documented.

When you have a job, you have a process. You get up, eat, exercise, go to work, attend meetings, and on and on. If are not disciplined in career transition, you could miss a networking event, skip your meditation that day, and it could affect your mood, or worse yet, cause you to forget an interview.

My calendar was fuller during my career transitions with morning rituals (exercise, meditation), networking, part-time jobs, etc. than when I was working. It did keep me on schedule and enable me to get it all done. When you're in transition, you cumulate the functions of administrative assistant, physical trainer, janitor, etc. You need something to help you stay organized, and keep you on schedule.

CHAPTER 2
Much-Needed Tools for Success

Read, create and use every one of these "tools":
- Elevator Pitch vs. Value Proposition
- Value Proposition
- LinkedIn
- Resume
- Business Cards
- Networking/Marketing Tools
- Templates/Standard Forms
- Preparing for the Long Haul
- Control What You Can Control
- Get a Library Card

Elevator Pitch vs. Value Proposition Statement?

Although many books, coaches, etc., point out the benefits and needs for an "Elevator Pitch," I have never been a fan of it. At the position level I was seeking, the "Elevator Pitch" was too long, and thus the interviewer tended to lose interest. I found that my "Value Proposition Statement" was more in tune with my style, perhaps because I am so direct. Also, during interviews, your interviewer or new networking person typically has little time, and quickly wants to get to the bottom line.

If you can't tell who you are, what you are capable of, and put forth the benefits you bring to your new company in two or three sentences, you don't really know what your true value is. Yes, creating a great Value Proposition statement will get your interviewer or networking person to want to know more about you. It will spark more discussion, they will spend more time with you, and basically give you more of what you are looking for.

Your Value Proposition Statement
The Value Proposition Statement is all about Who You Are. It reflects your intrinsic qualities, your values, your beliefs and passions. It connects you to the listener in the sense that you can allude to something that they may be seeking, and that you are the right person. For instance, during my first transition, I looked back and tried to find the one unique thing I had done better than anyone else before me. It was my ability to turn around flat or declining operations in record time, and provide the bottom-line results.

My Value Proposition Statement was something like this:

> *"I am a military veteran and business executive with 18 years' experience in global operations. I have a proven ability to make stagnant or declining companies competitive again, with experience in four major industries: RFID (Embedded Technology), Electronics Assembly, Industrial Automation, and Automotive."*

These two sentences come off my tongue in less than 20 seconds. They bring in my military career and leadership abilities, my fields of experience, my action/passion, and also the industries that are relevant to the person I am speaking with. Take what you are known for and bring it down to the shortest, most impactful and energetic message; then own it. *Do not hesitate to state it; it is who you are, your core in business. No one can take it away from you.*

The right people will connect with it; they will want to know more about you. It's meant to draw them in, and if you do it right, you will create followers/supporters. If an "Elevator Pitch" is your verbal resume, then your Value Proposition is your summary page. The Elevator Pitch is all about you and what you have done, and if you haven't aligned it with the potential employer you are meeting/networking with, you force them to try to process your past and how that relates to what they need or are searching for—and that may complicate things for you. On the other hand, a Value Proposition expressed properly, combined with some homework on the potential employer or network member you are meeting with, can really hit them in the pockets, as it relates to sales, profitability, etc. Again, *don't be shy about stating with confidence what makes you better or unique in your field of expertise,* compared to your competition.

LinkedIn

• • •

TIPS AND STRATEGIES:

Based on my experience, most of your traffic will come from LinkedIn, so you will need to make sure your LinkedIn profile is optimized.

This goes way beyond just listing the titles and experience you may have had in the past, and should focus on your brand. Broadcasting what makes you unique is critical because somewhere out there someone is searching for you. If your profile is not optimal and branded to you personally, it will become lost in a sea of millions, and require more time for your next employer to find you.

With branding all the rage now, it is absolutely critical that your personal brand come through clearly on your LinkedIn profile. It can take time to optimize your profile, and I suggest hiring a professional for branding, and for your LinkedIn profile. I won't go much into detail here, as there are many excellent books about this topic and able professionals who can help you in this regard. I can tell you though that *branding is essential when it comes to standing out and differentiating yourself from other professionals.* As the famous Oscar Wilde saying goes: "Be yourself, because everyone else is taken." Add a little personality to it as well because it could be the differentiator that will allow you to link up with your next employer.

As an example, before my LinkedIn profile was improved by one of these experts, between 70–80 people were looking at my profile at any given 90-day period. After her magic, and now going on four years, the number of my profile views hasn't fallen below 1,500 views every 90 days.

Talking with a CEO in transition recently, I asked him what makes him unique. "Well, I was the CEO of a $XXX-million-dollar company..." My response to him was: so are the six other men/women in the waiting room for the next interview. *What is the unique Super Power that you possess over everyone else in the waiting line? That is the core of your brand. Get it, develop it, enhance it and build on it.*

Resume

Pretty much like everything else while you are in transition, your resume needs a new look. This is not to say that you need to spend hundreds or a thousand dollars for someone to redo it for you. Chances are you haven't updated it since the last time you landed a job; whether that was a few years ago or more than a decade ago.

You will need several versions of your resume, and each should be comprised of two parts:

1. A top page with general highlights, which I would describe as the page that sparks enough curiosity for the reader to want to reach back out to you, and find out more about you. You can use this page as a networking reference or a cursory introduction to a potential connection or recruiter. Do not try to fit your entire history and education (and end up using a 6-point font size). If you do, you will both miss the point, and also not get a response. This specific page again should highlight the highest two-to-four accomplishments that you have achieved in the most recent position you've held, and should point out how it relates to the reader/recruiter you are addressing. For the position you held before your last one, you should describe one-to-two high achievements, maximum. And for the remaining positions (10 years max of your career), just list the respective position/title, company and years.

2. This one should be your detailed resume, with a maximum of two-to-three pages. Following the outline above you should be able to have a really good one with a short summary that highlights a detailed Value Proposition that is aligned with the job you are seeking. You may want to ensure that your past job titles are in line with current trends, and not age you out of the opportunity. Also, make sure that the results you list are your highest achievements, and do not overload the resume with so much information that the viewer/recruiter feels like you have revealed everything—and does not call you back.

If you are looking at a few opportunities in different fields, say in Operations and another in Sales, you may want to have a separate resume for each. After you are done with them, you may want to ask a friend or two to review them. Because I am not a particularly good wordsmith, I need a second pair of eyes checking my spelling and sentence structure. I am sure with the current network base you are now a part of, you can get someone to review your resumes, give you some free advice, and reduce your chances of getting tossed in the trash for misspelled words, etc.

It is not absolutely necessary to get your resume professionally done, with all kinds of free resources online. It pays to search Google for resume templates, examples, etc. that will help you get further ahead than if you try to create it yourself, without help.

Finally, you should have an Executive Bio. This is very useful for executive networking, as it gives the reader a profile of you that is clear and concise with details that might not be brought out in a resume or come up in an initial network meeting.

The executive bio is more than your Value Proposition and less than your resume. It's considered your marketing tool; just enough to whet the appetite while not giving away the entire recipe. It's a one-page culmination of your experience, skill, and brand.

You have to start with an earth-shattering introduction summary of what makes you unique and different than anyone else in your field/position. I looked at it like this: as if I was interviewing you, and six more people were in the waiting room. What could you say that would tell me I had no need to interview the others?

Then create highlights in a bullet format that leads to the future question of "Tell me how you did these tremendous feats." Again, give them enough that makes them want more. Like your resume, it should align with the potential needs of the person on the other side of the table—so you need to do your research.

As this is not your resume, do not forget to use your marketing side to incorporate a few (not to many) colored small standard forms/graphs that show substantial improvements under your leadership/time within those organizations.

Remember this is your marketing tool that leaves them wanting more and gets you in the hiring processes.

Business Cards

This is a must when you are networking. Although business cards are kind of an old-fashioned way to identify yourself, they are still a requirement in the business world. An exchange of business cards just makes it easier when you are networking, and the CEO or President of a company asks, "Do you have a business card?" You should always have some at the ready, and hand out one, or better yet two (for possible distribution to a contact of theirs). You can have a personal one or include a business that is a part of your overall brand. For example, if you are doing consulting, hold interim management positions, etc. it can be a great way to help start a part-time business, as well as in your search for a good landing.

Order at least 250 business cards before you start networking, and with all your current contact information, which may have to be adjusted during your transition. Many sites like "VistaPrint" offer high-quality business cards at a very low cost.

What should be on the business card? Your name, contact information, a title if you would like (even if you are unemployed) can be the same one you recently had or are searching to land. If you have a marketing background or a contact, you may be able to put a brand logo or a picture.

Network Card/Marketing Tool

I found that many executives use a one-page resume or summary page for both the purpose of networking and introductory interviews. However, I later noticed that a high percentage of people folded that one page and placed it in "the book of no return." By that I mean, out of sight out of mind, eventually later ending up in the garbage at the office or at home.

I took the 8.5" x 11" page format and turned it into a 4.25" x 11" concept, which I call the "Network Card." Instead of regular paper, I used heavier card stock to give it some weight and make it more difficult to fold. Placed in their planner/book my profile would stick out, and give them a constant reminder of our meeting. During my transitions, I pulled the golden nuggets out of each meeting and networking event and put them into this "Network Card." (See example below)

George Murray

Chief Operating Officer • President • Vice President

- *Business & Sales Growth • Net & EBITDA Improvement*
- *International Operations*

763-688-1875 • georgecmurray@gmail.com

• www.linkedin.com/in/georgecmurray

WHAT CAN YOU EXPECT FROM ME:

- **I** — *I* can really learn from others; this is my hands on approach
- **N** — *N*ever let setbacks dampen my enthusiasm; high energy
- **S** — *S*how people that obstacles can be overcome-teamwork
- **P** — *P*eoples attitude can change others thinking; continuous improvement
- **I** — *I*nject a sense of purpose in all we do; cheerleader
- **R** — *R*emember inspiration works better with perspiration; not afraid of hard work
- **E** — *E*njoy the fruits of ones labor; creating an environment where people want to come to work

GOAL:

Secure a C-level position within a $20-$250M company that require a strategic, servant leader to drive growth in both sales and net profit:

Would consider: Vice President/General Manager of Larger Division of multiple manufacturing sites with P&L responsibility

Industry type: Manufacturing, Automotive, Electronic design/manufacturing, Industrial automation, medical manufacturing, machining manufacturing, Telecommunications, software and IT security

EXPERTISE & KNOWLEDGE:

◄ Global Marketing Strategies & Growth	◄ Profit/Loss Leadership	◄ Transformational Change
◄ New Business Development	◄ Turnarounds & Restructures	◄ Vision/Mission Alignment
◄ Global Manufacturing Operations	◄ EBITDA Improvement	◄ Operational Excellence
◄ Sales & Revenue Leadership	◄ New Product Launch	◄ Mergers & Acquisitions

I used my LinkedIn profile picture so first and foremost people could make an immediate connection between my LI profile and the contact information on my Network card. However, the front page of the card emphasizes what I could do for them—because at that point it's all about them. How can I help them? What skills do they need? What potential need might they have—or their critical needs, and how can you outline those in skillsets you have. What potential need might they have? The front page is definitely all about them, and conducive to matching my skills and attributes with what they need or the needs of.

The backside of the card is a brief description of your skills, education, and work experience. It reinforces the front side, where you list potential needs, through examples of work history, etc. Also, for the benefit of your fellow network members, it lists companies or people you are trying to connect with. Finally, you can use the back side of the card to identify certain industries, companies, or individuals that you are the most interested in connecting with, and give them a checklist for their convenience.

You should try to differentiate yourself from the competition in many ways, and the Network Card is but one example of how to do that. I saw less than five percent of people in transition use this tool.

Templates

If you are doing things right, a career transition can be a very busy time, what with networking, interviewing, calls, etc. It's also a time when certain things can easily be overlooked if you do not have tracking tools in the form of templates/standardized forms. Templates can be used as a standard tracking tool, and also save you lots of time while you are busy searching for your next position.

- **Recruiter/Interview:** The purpose of my first template was to control all Recruiter/Interview activities. Although it is a spreadsheet template, it is a great tool to make sure you do all the proper follow-up and track the progress of all your contacts with hiring managers and recruiters. There is a slot for each contact person with their email address, phone number, etc. Additionally, it has their title, salary range of the position (if known), and space for a brief update after each meeting or call to keep things fresh in your mind. Have it in front of you when you call for an update. Recruiters in particular are dealing with multiple candidates all the time—and you don't want to fall through the cracks.
- **LinkedIn Introductions:** The next template was a few LinkedIn introductions. Depending on the level of the person you are trying to reach, for instance CEO, Director, Manager, etc., you may want to use different templates that clearly state your Value Proposition in just a few words. To save time, you may want to initially set aside a few hours to enable cutting and pasting repetitive information (make sure you change the name of the recipient, though, before hitting send!).

One of my examples:

> *I'd like to introduce myself. My name is George Murray. I am a military veteran and business executive with 18 years of experience leading global operations and manufacturing at multiple sites. I have expertise in the Automotive, Electronics, Industrial Automation, and High Technology industries.*

Remember that you have only 300 characters (above is 294) to make a first impression and be unique.

Again, LinkedIn is a great resource with which to communicate with your many connections. I even developed a few birthday response templates. Not just the standard Happy Birthday wishes you can click on in LinkedIn, but the kind that sent the recipient genuine birthday wishes, giving the impression that you really cared about them, personalized the wishes and giving them a brief update. That's a great way to stay at the top of their mind and have many people help you look for that new position.

Birthday Wish example:
May you achieve much more than you already have in each of the birthdays ahead. Warm greetings and best wishes for your birthday. I hope to hear from you soon as I am looking for a new role/career and would love to talk to you about any ideas you may have.
—George 952-XXX-XXXX

- **Connection Acceptance:** Finally, you need a template for responding to those who accept your request to connect. I believe that in order to set yourself apart, you need to respond relatively quickly (less than 36 hours). The feedback should be just a few lines thanking them for their time and consideration, and perhaps finishing with an insightful question. This should prompt them to continue the dialogue with a response. However, do not get upset if they don't reply; I have had a response rate of only about 40 percent. But here again you have a chance to make a good first impression, in contrast to the majority of job seekers that do not go the extra mile. Don't forget to change the name if your template has a name on the intro; it would be more than a bit embarrassing if you sent it to Barney while it was meant for Fred.

- **Prepare for the Long Haul**

Even in a great economy, it will take you a while to land your position. Sure, if you want to get a $12/hour job it won't take you long.

However, any professional position is going to take a while, and a great deal of effort.

One year after landing my newest position, I have consistently kept networking with a high percentage of people in transition. Much like I once did myself, the majority of these people felt that it would take only a few months at most to land a new position, but that is a big mistake. Plenty of professional positions are obtained by means of references, recommendations, and introductions. If you want one of those positions, and develop a greater ability to find your next big opportunity, it is critical that you start networking and come up with a plan to get the most out of your network.

Certain things in life are absolutely critical, but unfortunately, we have to learn somewhat on our own because school does not teach them. Interviewing, balancing a checkbook, and networking for your next opportunity are among those.

- **Review Your Financial Situation:** Part of preparing for your new job search is to review your financial situation with your spouse or significant other. Do this after a week or two of decompression and getting past the frustration, etc. from being laid off, fired, or from a reduction in workforce, etc. Do a review of your family finances, much like a business scrutinizes all its expenses when times are tough. It's "You Inc.," and to tell you the truth, it has always been this way, but you are only realizing it now. Companies own the titles; you own your career.

Review all expenses! For example, there are services during winter months *to assist you with your bills if you live in a cold climate/state.* Also, reach out to certain vendors and rein in your costs, for example renegotiate your internet and cable bills, which can easily save you $100–

$150 dollars a month. Honestly, it's something you should do periodically anyway, perhaps every three to five years. As a loyal customer you should get a large discount, and if not, then change service providers.

Ditto for your gym membership, as another example. I had a health club membership that was like a large car payment. To keep my commitment to finally getting in shape and lose weight, I switched to a simple gym membership for only $19.95/month, another few hundred dollars savings.

Believe me, we, and especially my wife, became very skilled at cutting costs.

Control What You Can Control

√ Stop the Bleeding

Part of being humble in transition is trying to reduce your outflow of money. The great thing about a good economy is that there are plenty of jobs; however, the majority of them seem to pay in the $12–$18 range. Nothing is really beneath you when you are in job transition, and are looking for ways to slow the burn of your money.

Regardless of whatever severance package you may receive initially (meaning you sign these papers and we will give you an amount for a certain time), unemployment compensation, etc., your income will almost certainly decrease while in transition. You must reduce your cashflow to a minimum, as the spigot of money slows down to a trickle or gets cut off altogether. Along with finding your next career opportunity, you must simultaneously find ways to reduce your expenses and find interim sources of income.

One way to do the latter is to work part-time while you continue to network, interview, and look for a new opportunity. This can be assuming a lower position, taking on a temporary job, consulting, etc. This helps not only financially, but is also good for the mind. It reminds you that you have other skills that are needed. It also enables you to network with people you may have never have been exposed to, and who might help you get closer to your goal.

During my first transition, I took on a supervisor position at a local store that was looking for someone to manage their plumbing department. I learned more about plumbing in four months from a couple of men who worked there than I did in my previous 40 years of life. One man was a 20-year career employee who really knew where everything was in the store. Another was a retired plumber, and just by listening to how he troubleshot customer problems, I not only learned how to address my own plumbing challenges at home but became better skilled at helping customers when the other two men were not in the store. My customer service interface abilities improved immensely and helped me further my career by making it easier for me to get out there, talk to people and help them overcome challenges. A very rewarding experience, indeed.

Additionally, I worked a stint at an Amazon distribution center, 12-hour shifts on Thursday, Friday and Saturday nights. I hadn't worked the third shift in over 15 years. Additionally, in an effort to lose weight and be in better health, I ran five to seven miles a day during that time and did approximately 20,000 steps every day. During a 12-hour shift, I managed to get to 25-30,000 steps! Talk about challenging... doing all that while most people were sleeping between 2–5 a.m. It proved to me that nothing is really beneath me. I was motivated to provide for my family, and prove to myself that I could still do it. This is where humility and being humble trumps status or the way people view you. They are not going to pay your bills at the end of the day. Challenge yourself often, continue to learn, and be the best you can be. As you look for your next career opportunity, and need to slow the cash burn, don't discount a temporary or part time job in the short term. The Army taught me very young, "I may lose my job and struggle, but I can still clean a mean toilet, and mop and buff a floor like glass."

I continue to work a part-time job to replenish our savings and help pay for my kids' college (it's now close to two years after landing my full-time position), so I don't have to draw more from my slim savings. As I work my current role in my new executive position, I have also worked for two years at a high-end clothing store, replenishing the money I've lost during the last two career transitions. It always amazes me when people talk to me about work ethic, hard work, determination, etc.—I just smile. Along the way I also met a few professionals in career transition who had been at very senior levels in their careers, taking on similar short-term positions.

I met a career executive with a Ph.D., who was struggling to find his next position. During his time in transition, he worked for FedEx, an incredibly humbling thing for this lofty degree holder. Has it ever occurred to you that the person who delivered your last package may have a Ph.D.? Perhaps he's not in a career transition, but maybe looking to pay for his kids' college so his children don't have to go into debt or he doesn't have to take from his retirement accounts?

Remember, there are ways to stop the bleeding, as long as you stay humble.

This approach not only helps reduce the cash burn from your savings/retirement/etc., it also gives you a sense of purpose, you feel more productive, and feel good about interacting with others. These are all things we tend to lose when we are out of work because all our friends, relatives, and work associates are working during the day while we sit at the kitchen table, worrying about what we should do.

Psychological Effect of Transition

It is not a subject taught in school, or anywhere else for that matter. Namely how a job loss, layoff, etc. is likely to severely affect your mood and mindset. It comes as a shock to our psyche while all our friends and work associates are busy in their daily work life, while we sit alone and contemplate the next steps for weeks, months, and sometimes even years.

When our daily routine is brutally interrupted by a job loss, we can easily get a dark path of depression, self-doubt, and despair. I have seen the proverbial "Eeyores" out there feeling this way. When you peel back their onion skin, you find out that they do not have a daily routine, don't eat well, don't exercise, and don't sleep well. I found all of these are critical elements to put yourself in a better frame of mind going forward.

Below are a few ways to optimize your mind for success in transition:

- **Journaling:**

One way to get it all out of your head and onto paper is journaling. *Write about* your feelings, goals, aspirations, frustrations, etc., and keeping a record of your days was also very helpful. First, I wanted to outline five things each day that I was thankful for, for example my family, good health or a recent positive event. When you look at life that way instead of just your current professional situation, it really puts you in a better frame of mind. It may also inspire you, and perhaps gives you an idea for one or two things that you would want to accomplish that day or week.

Again, when we have goals, we have something to look forward to, and it puts us in a positive, forward-thinking mindset. Things that we can look forward to, and we are able to achieve within a certain timeframe, *have a way to lift your spirits and give you a positive outlook.*

Let's face it, the hardships of life can get you down real fast, and even faster during a career transition, when you don't have much of a focus or things to look forward to. I found journaling to have a great effect on my sense of accomplishment for the day or the week, and the ability to get it on paper to go back and review was quite helpful. Our minds don't remember everything, so journaling is a great way to record it.

Finally, I always jotted down two-to-three things I aspired to do, was able to do, or even as a challenge to see if I could accomplish them in the future. These items, by the way, can provide input data for your Vision Board, something I will talk about later in this book.

During your career transition, you normally have a lot of time, but, as I said earlier, if you are not using it wisely, it can all go to waste. The more I learned during my career transition, the more I realized the importance of daily journaling—basically jotting down your thoughts of the day, ideas, and things to be thankful for each day.

Thoughts were mainly about how I felt each day—happy, sad, confused, etc. It helped getting it out and on paper. My journal was almost like a psychologist that didn't talk back. It was therapeutic in a way, to get your feelings on paper. A transition can really be lonely and depressing at times. You don't want to put any more stress on your relationships with friends and family than they can handle, and journaling helps get it off your chest.

Ideas means writing down at least one or two concepts for the day. It could be starting a business, or developing the next widget, or even writing a book. Imagine, if you wrote one or two ideas each day for a year, you could potentially have *over 700 new ideas*. Kind of like brainstorming if you were a business. As I came to learn, you are the CEO of "You, Inc.," and if you're not strategizing and brainstorming for new ideas, your competition will be, and will beat you tomorrow (as in getting the job that was meant for you).

Things to be thankful for means listing the parts of your life you are grateful for each day. It is critical to pinpoint why you do what you do. You may go through a tough and lonely time, but you can't lose sight of your blessings in life, things you are truly thankful for. I found this can help when things look bleak.

Journaling can also be a testimony of the challenges you have faced and surmounted at the time (important, as our memory never gets better with age...), and can be used to reflect back later on what you did during this difficult time to overcome your challenges.

- **Get a Library Card**

Yes, they still have those and you would be surprised at the changes since you were at the library in your high school days. Most places that I researched *are free*. Or they charge a small amount, quite frankly an inexpensive investment for having access to a computer, a quiet place to do research, read, get information, assistance, and a place to go to besides your kitchen table or couch.

As I wrote earlier, you need a daily routine ("Day in the Life"). Part of that is getting up and getting out just like you would if you still had a regular job. Your most difficult job now is looking for a job when you're in a career transition.

You could schedule a meeting room at a lot of libraries. Librarians are "subject matter experts." Ask for their help in getting copies, scanning documents, etc. With all the assistance they can provide, why wouldn't you have a library card?

- **Set a Timeline:**

At the beginning of my second career transition I quickly set a timeline, like "I have to find a new opportunity before six months" (preferably *or less)*. Looking back at both transitions, I now realize that this was another painful lesson. My first transition took 13 months; not setting a timeline was a big reason why it took so long. Setting some kind of a timeline has a way to hold you accountable and stay on task. When you manage a project or set a goal for your team, you have to do the same thing. It also enables you to get certain new things done that you wouldn't necessarily do or think of doing without a timeline, like cold calling or sending introduction letters to strangers.

CHAPTER 3

Be the Boss of You: Create Your Routine, Your "Day in the Life" —and Live it

Create It—and Execute It:
If you don't create a routine for yourself, you will be meandering through much of the day and week. Before you know it, you will have wasted three months and accomplished little. What I am talking about here is the necessity to recreate your "Day in the Life."

A certain structure is important just about every day of your life; however, it is most critical during a transition. A common complaint we hear is that these people would like to sleep better, eat better, exercise more, etc. When you are busy working, these things may be easier said than done. When will we have time?

Your Time is Now! Invest in yourself *now!;* you have more than enough time. Devise a precise plan that will get you closer to your goals.

After a few weeks in transition, I looked at myself in the mirror—truly looked at myself. Then I said; "Who is going to hire this old, fat, ugly guy?" Well, I couldn't simply turn the clock back to when I was 25 or 30 years old. I couldn't really change much of my looks without spending a lot of money on plastic surgery. But I could take control of my weight. Like most people, I ate so poorly, and had progressively morphed into a sedative state as the years went by. Blame too many meetings for that.

So, one day I sat down and outlined all the things I wanted to change:

- Sleep better (more than four hours a night); this would help me not to look so tired, and could lift my droopy eyes, etc. I might even not look so ugly (joking again, but not so far from the truth).
- I could start walking (not entering a marathon right off, of course).
- After a good friend urged me to consider meditating, I took the plunge, and have made it a habit to meditate daily.
- Finally, I incorporated morning affirmations into my daily routine. Yes, I thought that affirmations were a bunch of nonsense. "I am successful, I am resourceful," etc. I was skeptical about this but found it was very good to keep a positive mindset). However, especially in transition, we can be our worst cheerleaders, and if we don't reinforce the good in our minds every day, we can turn negative. I looked at meditation to clear up all the cobwebs and negative thoughts, and then replaced them with positive thoughts and ideas through morning affirmations.

Thanks to this structure I became more confident, healthier, and happier each day. By extension I developed a more "can-do" attitude that showed at network meetings and whenever I interacted with people.

Instead of the "Eeyore" approach with an "Oh, woe is me" attitude, I was able to project a more confident, happy image of myself—and isn't that the type of person we all want to be around?

As a middle-aged executive, I knew that the competition was going to be fierce, but I found it was even more. With no time for self-reflection, with all the meetings, travel and lack of sleep, I saw a rundown, non-motivated, overweight person in the mirror. Yes, I can control that person in the mirror and fix what I have neglected for years. Start to sleep better, eat better, and exercise, starting slowly, and being committed will ensure your success. One weekend I outlined what changes I wanted to see in me, both personally and professionally.

> *"If you want to see a change in the world, start with yourself."*
> – Mahatma Gandhi

The power of sleep is an incredible advantage that I wasn't taking advantage of, and I wanted to change this. I believe when we make something important in our lives, we see a different perspective, which in turn can help you. I went from four hours a night on average to well over six hours in a few months just by changing my pattern. Go to bed at a set time each night, get ready for bed instead of just "jumping in"—at least have more of a winding-down process. This change gave me more energy and ability to focus than I have had in years.

• • •

TIPS AND STRATEGIES:

Lack of adequate sleep can affect many things in your life—energy throughout the day, memory, health, patience level, attitude about the world, and how you feel about yourself, just to name a few.

In seven months, I was able to lose 35-plus pounds, which meant that I looked better whenever I showed up for an interview. I made a better first impression; feeling better made me look better, and I felt that I was looked at in a much more positive light by others. Create your daily routine or "Day in the Life."

In transition you cannot control many things, for example, landing your new position, because the decision doesn't lie within you—but the way you progress through the day, as well as outlining your day for the best success in landing is. Setting your day up for success is the most important thing you have control over.

√ Health

Invest in a personal tracker device (Fitbit, Apple Watch, etc.) for better health, and track your steps, your calorie intake, and your sleep. *What we think we do, and what we do, can be unknown and far apart until we track it.* Speaking of health, if you are like me, sleep, exercise, and eating right always took somewhat of a backseat the past 10 years. Part of this whole process of career transition was reflecting what I had put on the backburner while "Life happened." Well, it happens whether you do or don't prioritize the things that are important in life. I learned in this process that *what you were is not what you have to be—so change it.* With all those commitments I had made to myself throughout those past years, now was the time to prioritize my things in my life.

• • •

TIPS AND STRATEGIES:

Living in a very visual world, and with first impressions being made in less than seven seconds—not leaving much time to say anything—you have to show up and be your best self.

For me, that meant getting on a regular exercise regimen. It's also important that you don't overload yourself. For example, start off by walking three miles, three times per week if you haven't done any exercise in month/years, and after four-to-six weeks, add a mile. Then start to run down the hills on those walks or run between every other light pole. Before you know it, in just a few months you have a continuous jog going.

I didn't just start running, which would have been both depressing and cause another health issue immediately. However, I started walking. Do you know that the average person walks only 5,000 steps per day (close to 2,000 steps in a 5,280-foot mile)? Getting out and walking three to five miles each morning, I was 15,000 steps ahead of the average person.

After a few months, I was awkwardly trotting, and a few more months, I was running. Then I focused on reducing my intake of sugar, the most addictive thing on this planet that is cheap, easy-to-get, and in most any food on your plate. As an example, I calculated that with two teaspoons of sugar in my coffee each morning, I was eating three pounds of sugar each year. Slowly backing off having sugar in my coffee over a few months, I was able to eliminate that much sugar. I also stopped drinking calories like in lemonade, and non-diet sodas, and drinking nothing but water or unsweetened tea. That reduced another 20 pounds of sugar (on the low side) a year. I was able to reduce my sugar intake over 23 pounds in two areas, and with more activity, I dropped the weight.

My last quest during the transition to the health improvement movement was to consistently get better sleep. Since my military days, on average I haven't slept for more than 4.5 hours each night. This isn't good on my weight nor on my heart, so I wanted to find ways to get better sleep. Researching and looking up better ways came down to the basics. I am an early riser (thank you Uncle Sam) so I needed to consistently go to bed earlier. Another reason to have that tracker device is it can remind you, no matter where you are, it's time to shut the day down, and it can also track your deep sleep, REM sleep, etc. In six months, I was up to six hours a night, and my energy and outlook on life had improved tremendously. I am sure my heart thanked me as well.

What health improvements have you wanted to change? Do it today, and do it consistently.

√ Musical Mantra

The right music can motivate you. It might be that song from your high school years, a vivid time in your past, or something motivational that can get you in the right mindset. Using music can help bring you out of a rut, help you move forward, and can get you to run that extra mile.

• • •

TIPS AND STRATEGIES:

Whether you work out, run or stretch, you can use the music to start your day and start putting you in the right frame of mind.

For over 25 years, I have started each morning with the song "Thunderstruck" by AC/DC. To help paint a picture, the song came out in 1991 when I was serving in the Army in Desert Storm. We were on the battlefield in Saudi Arabia awaiting orders from President Bush to cross over and engage the enemy.

Most of us had a "boom box" in our M1/A1 Abrams tank, and for those who are in the digital age, it was this huge electronic unit with speakers and a cassette tape. Imagine this: the Army was spread over seven miles deep and 22 miles wide of military armor ready to cross over the border into Iraq. Blasting this song, imagining how could we fail? Well, we didn't. Music is inspiring, it gives you memories, and it can drive you.

As part of my day, I had a musical mantra with that song, along with others that helped me keep going. Another song that kept me sane and instilled a sense of "all will turn out well" was Louis Armstrong's "What a Wonderful World." Yes, music can help in these times and elsewhere to keep you motivated, inspired, and driven. It was part of my playlist on my Spotify when I ran each morning.

Whatever your choice of music, put songs together that get you motivated and energized, and keep you on a personal high so you can take on each day.

√ Affirmations

One day, someone introduced me to affirmations. Being a highly skeptical man from Connecticut and Army-trained individual, I thought these "I am" were all fluff and crazy stuff. Lisa, a friend of mine through transition, told me straight. "Try it for 30 days; then tell me you're not going to do it."

Using affirmations now, I can tell you it has changed my view on life. When we are in transition, we can tend to be our worst cheerleaders—

and we really do need someone to pull out the person inside of us that is willing to work harder. I have selected 10 (of the 15 below) that I repeat daily, and they motivated me right before I went out each day for networking and interviewing.

You can also post them on a mirror, computer/home office, or in your car. Constant reminders that *You are successful, You are a master sales woman/man, You are too great to settle for less, You can create a better future*, etc. My first thought had been: you can't be serious, but yes, affirmations help by reinforcing the positive mindset.

Click here to download your FREE copy of affirmation sensation: https://motivationping.com/affirmations/#:~:text=%20Positive%20Affirmations%20That%20Work%20Fast%20In%202020,I%20believe%20in%20myself.%20I%20can...%20More%20

Try these helpful affirmations:
1. "I have the knowledge to make smart decisions for myself."
2. "I have all that I need to make today a great day."
3. "I am, and always will be, enough."
4. "I acknowledge my own self-worth—my confidence is rising."
5. "I let go of any negative feelings about myself or my life, and accept all that is good."
6. "I always attract only the best of circumstances, and I have the best, positive people in my life."
7. "I am courageous. I am willing to act and face my fears."
8. "I have unlimited power."
9. "I am a powerful creator. I create the life I want, and I enjoy it."
10. "Every day I discover interesting and exciting new paths to pursue."
11. "I trust my intuition, and I always make wise decisions."
12. "I am focused on my goals and feel passionate about my work."
13. "I work well under pressure and always feel motivated."

14. "I am living to my full potential."
15. "I have everything I need to face any obstacles that come."

• • •

TIPS AND STRATEGIES:

Continue using affirmations beyond your transition; change them up as necessary to keep you motivated and have an edge.

Use Your Past to Fuel Your Future—in a positive way
You will survive, although at times when it feels like the world is against you, you must find the way to persevere. I could use my past to motivate me and keep me moving forward. I grew up in a low-income style: my dad had an 8th-grade education and worked at a foundry for 30 years and was a car mechanic on the weekends. My mother had a 10th-grade education, and worked at a retail store that has long been gone, and she drove a taxi on the weekends. It taught me that you do *whatever it takes to survive, provide, and move forward.*

Then my sister passed away around my sixth birthday; she was such a little lady, with dresses, make-believe, and a smile. She was born with a heart defect, and when she was three-and-a-half years old, God took her to be with him. It was the only time I ever saw my father cry. It taught me that life is not always easy, and you need to smile even in tough times—and yes, it's okay to cry.

Then my parents divorced when I was 11, and it was not a friendly one. Like most kids, I didn't understand what I did wrong; why didn't my father want to visit us anymore? It taught me that sometimes love cannot conquer all—and that is okay.

I was bullied most of my school years, and one bully was going into the Army the same time I was, and he was telling me I wasn't tough enough (you can imagine). All my time in basic I heard his words and used them to motivate myself. I found out later that I made it through basic training, but he didn't. It taught me two things: 1) You can do whatever you set your mind to do, and 2) Don't let negative people trespass into your mind.

Then I received orders for Desert Shield/Desert Storm toward the end of my service agreement that had been extended, and I was flown to Saudi Arabia. I was in a few situations that if I hadn't overcome, I wouldn't be writing this book today. It taught me that life will not always be easy—and there are always ways to overcome adversity.

Hey, everyone has had obstacles that they have overcome in life. I have learned to positively use those failures and challenges to motivate myself forward.

• • •

TIPS AND STRATEGIES:

Whoever you share your life with—it's important to increase your daily communication. Now is when you need to talk things through...together, and agree upon solutions.

Don't Forget Your Spouse (and Kids, etc.)
You might be busier now than before when you had a full-time job. Don't forget to put time to connect, discuss, and share ideas on your "Day in the Life" schedule. It also can be a very stressful time, out of work with little-to-no income, money issues can put a strain on relationships. You need to discuss all the topics: Kids, Money, Bills, Finance, etc.

openly and without frustration and stress. *This can be borderline difficult.* Whether you are the major breadwinner or helping create the best life; you need to sit down and outline some game rules. Stress, loss of a job, etc. can put a wedge between you and others if you don't talk about how you're feeling and what you are doing. Typically, I had gone to my job, did my work, and came home. Now my wife had more stress and worry than ever because we were without an income, and all the expenses built up very quickly.

Set a particular time, whether it's at the end of the day after networking, before dinner, or later before bed. Talk it out, keep positive, but do share concerns; it may just bring you closer together. I know it did me, and through it all, my wife was such a strong "coach" for the family.

If you have kids, it can be difficult for the younger ones to understand. However, I learned it was important to be honest, open, and positive. They may have no questions, some questions, or a lot of questions. But try to keep it positive and upbeat, because kids can take it personally as they may think that they did something wrong—or the stress can create problems for them at school. But for them it's also a learning experience. The good thing is they are watching and learning, and if they see you down, depressed, and discouraged, it can quickly show them *what not to do.* Telling them about your process in very simple and basic words, as well as showing your confidence about finding employment—and that it will take time, will reassure them.

You know your family better than I do; this is just a suggestion. It's what I did, and found it was a much better experience by being open with them early rather than later. Our children found out things by observing—meaning that you're not going to work before they go to school, or you are dressing up more than you used to and staying late and missing dinner.

· · ·

TIPS AND STRATEGIES:

Kids are smart, smarter than you think, and treating them with respect, and letting them know what is going on, is a learning and teaching opportunity.

Be the Student

In transition, you have a lot of time, which is both bad and good. *Bad* is that there is little-to-no money coming in. *Good* is what we are outlining in this book as well as continuing your education, whether it is a certificate, finish up a degree, starting a Masters, or reading to keep up with your industry or the industries you're interested in.

One of the first questions you are asked in the interviewing process is: "What have you been doing to keep up with the industry, etc.," and you want to say more than "Applying to jobs on the job boards." That interview will not progress. Be a lifelong learner, I say. Do a few courses, if you can handle the workload. Go to the library and find books in new leadership shifts, finances or financial review of companies, or listening, as examples.

· · ·

TIPS AND STRATEGIES:

*We could all use better listening skills,
especially if you're looking for a new leadership role.*

Do a bit of research, some states have state-funded programs for those in career transition. In my home state of Minnesota, I used *Hired.org*. As their website states: "*Hired* is a vital part of the metropolitan Twin Cities. They support individuals and families so they can learn new skills and achieve their academic and career goals."

I was able to complete my Mini-Master's program in Project Management that costs thousands of dollars, which they paid. Their services also included classes in Personal Branding, and improving your LinkedIn profile. I highly recommend attending classes like these if you need to get traffic to your profile. As Kathleen Crandall's trademarked quotation about branding asks, "What are you known for, and what happens because of you?" ™

So much help exists out there, and as part of your networking, discussed later in this book, should be a question on what other programs/services are available. By the way, *Hired.org* will assist if you have a bill that is inhibiting you from getting to networking or interviews, such as automotive repairs.

• • •

TIPS AND STRATEGIES:

Be a student, a life-long learner during your transition time—and continue learning all kinds of new things for the rest of your life.

YouTube was My Personal Coach

While you are in transition you are always finding ways to keep costs down. YouTube became a valuable resource in so many ways: learning, motivation, inspiration, and relaxing, just to name a few.

For my health, each morning after a run I was able to use different videos to both meditate and for my morning affirmations—to clear the cobwebs and set my mind full of positive reinforcement for the day. I would search for a topic like "meditation for positive energy," and poof, there was a resource of videos that would take me through my mediation, whether I wanted 10 minutes, 20 minutes, or longer.

• • •

TIPS AND STRATEGIES:

Each day on YouTube I had a different focus, and it was like a personal coach who I was able to get for free.

I learned how to better position my LinkedIn profile and my resume to both drive traffic and improve my branding, which are critical among the sea of competition. I had scheduled, again on my calendar, 20–30 minutes some time each week to review videos on topics such as "Improving LinkedIn traffic, Increasing Likes/Shares/Comments, and Postings that get the most responses." Along with that, I did searches on YouTube for best resumes for executives and professionals.

I discovered that you also could learn while you sleep with sleep hypnosis. A few times a month, I would listen to a topic at a low volume, such as "overcoming adversity," or "positive motivation," and put my earbuds in and fall asleep.

Finally, I regularly scheduled some time to follow certain people to keep up to date and relevant on topics such as Leadership and Employee Development like Tony Robbins, Simon Sinek, Jocko Wollink, and Simon Gray (*UK-Career Codex*). Not only were they motivational, but they reinforced and helped me improve my leadership and interviewing skills, and improved me personally.

Stop/Start/Continue Model

Much like work, where we need to always review progress and adjust accordingly, career transition is no different. If we do not put a line in the sand at some frequency—setting a time every three to four weeks to review our progress can very quickly pass by with little attempts to adjust things for the better. Seven months into my first 13-month transition, I came upon another tidbit of valuable information. Every third or fourth Saturday at 7:30 a.m.–8:15 a.m. on my calendar (as a reminder) I would evaluate what was working (Continue doing); what was not working (Stop doing). Finally, I would leave 15 minutes to brainstorm things I could start doing I wasn't doing yet. For example, cold calling executives and leaving a powerful introduction and my contact information.

• • •

TIPS AND STRATEGIES:

Do not fail: Every three to four weeks, you must evaluate your progress.

- **Evaluate your progress**: I came to understand that you must be able to evaluate your progress—and every three to four weeks I blocked time out in my calendar (usually early Saturday mornings) before the family woke up—and evaluated my overall progress in the recent past. This is the process.

- **Review what you are doing:** I would review what things were going well, like was I getting in front of people, as well as keeping positive and full of energy. Could I stop things that were not going well or not working, which could include reaching out directly (don't knock it till you try it), or your direct LinkedIn introduction. Evaluate it like you are someone who was going to meet you for the first time, or interview you. Are you able to identify and verbalize the three to four lines that make you unique, compared to the other 100 people with a similar background or skill?

- **Start something new:** Finally, start something new; like going direct on LinkedIn to hiring managers or CEOs. Again, make sure your message is concise and unique because you have only 300 characters on LinkedIn to introduce yourself, so make it count. Some argue that there is not enough space to properly introduce yourself. I learned that it forces you to think differently—because an introduction is not all about you, especially when you are trying to get noticed/liked. Those 300 characters forced me to look at myself a bit differently. Additionally, as we live in a world that has a very short attention span, you just have less than 30 seconds to impress others/introduce yourself. *Make it unique.* One introduction I used when I was asked face to face from a CEO or Board member, "tell me about yourself" was:

> *I am a Rappel Master.... (Wait 3 seconds for that quirk facial expression—deciphered what the ...?) Much like my military career, I drop into difficult situations, assess the team, develop a strategy collaboratively, and execute the plan.*

You can say, "Oh, that is a play on words, or that is cute, etc." However, you have a short window to make an impact. You need to make yourself unique and memorable. Very few are going to remember the statement, "I have over 20 years' experience... wah, wah, wah." But they will remember that "Rappel Master" analogy long after they leave the coffee shop or that network event where they heard over 30 long speeches.

The Value Proposition above took me about four hours to develop, and it outlines what I have been doing for the past 15 years—turning companies around profitably by jumping in, engaging with teams, understanding the obstacles, and collectively developing plans to improve using accountability milestones.

Another one I used to go direct to people for LinkedIn introductions:

I'd like to introduce myself, George Murray. I am a military veteran and business executive with 18 years of experience leading global operations and manufacturing at multiple sites. Expertise in Automotive, Electronics, Industrial Automation, and High Technology industries.

Writing this one took me about an hour, and it clearly and briefly outlines my military, leadership background, as well as the industries I worked in, all in 38 words! Yes, my whole two-and-a-half-page resume in 38 words. Try it, and make it happen.

- **Video Blog (VLOG)**

Speaking about starting something new, what about making a video blog of your entire career transition. Share one-minute videos each day, for example, on a topic, or on overcoming some adversity, or just your feelings for the day, or an area of the business that you look to improve, with suggestions and metrics. You would think it may sound funny, that no one would be interested, etc. Think again.

Someone recommended I start making and then posting short videos on LinkedIn about a topic, whether it related to this book or a way I improved business. When I was reminded to be short and concise on the message, I replied: who would want to hear that? Funny thing: quite a few of my first shaky, nervous video received over 5,000 views, and I was more than shocked. As with anything you do, the messages get better, the dialogue more profound, and before too long you are a *semi*-professional video blogger. I stress on the word semi.

• • •

TIPS AND STRATEGIES:

Everyone has life experiences that can resonate with others. Your path and the way you have overcome obstacles can be a lesson for someone else.

You can also use it as a video diary of your journey, what things have you learned, and what have you overcome. The more you do it, you get better at it, and who knows, you may become the social media great that a lot of people will follow.

If you don't already have both a Twitter and Instagram account, I suggest creating one for your brand. For example, I have all my vlogs saved on: Get_Better_Start_Today on Instagram. It's another way to drive traffic, and to be unique and different. My vlogs are focusing the listener on ways to consider in order to get better in all areas of their life, health, business, etc. It's also a way for people to "Try it before they buy it" or before they meet you. This is a marketing way to tell people out in the social media world who you are and what drives you.

CHAPTER 4
Be Prepared: Every Networking Opportunity Counts

This chapter features these networking tips:
- Network Preparation
- Build Your Pipeline
- 10-10-10
- Network Events
- Top of Mind
- Energy
- Personal Board of Advisors

• Network Preparation – It's Not All About You

I often speak on this topic and truly believe the introduction/network meeting will get you the face-to-face meeting, but you truly have to find a way to build a relationship in a short period. I found if you approach the first meeting on a 70/30 split—that is letting them speak and talk about themselves 70 percent of the time—you will get/find a way to truly connect.

Do your homework the night before by reviewing their LinkedIn Profile, and you can find out common connections, perhaps a common school or previous company you worked at or did business with, as two examples. One of my first introductions/meetings I was able to learn that both his daughters went through college on swimming scholarships, and my daughter was currently swimming on her high school team. We spent 10 minutes just on that.

Since that meeting, we have introduced each other to more than three dozen executives/professionals. We truly connected. Finding a way that perhaps you can help them, like: is there a specific position that they are recruiting for (not what you are qualified for) you may help with? Perhaps they have a family trip coming up, and he wants some great advice on a restaurant that you know in the town they are vacationing.

• • •

TIPS AND STRATEGIES:

Once you give first or give often—people are more in favor of helping you later. When I realized it's not all about me, I became happier, I became more connected, and I became more sought-out.

One of the biggest learnings in my first transition was even though I had a great need to find a position to provide for my family, becoming truly rich was to learn from others, help others, and be present in the moment. When I started to realize it's not all about me, I became happier, I became more connected, and I became more sought out. *An older dog can learn new tricks as long as he or she is willing.*

- Showing up – the Way you Want to be Seen

One mistake during my first transition—I was showing up without "my brand." Sometimes I showed up in polo and dress pants; next time a shirt, tie, and dress slacks, and still another (mostly on Fridays, the dress-down day) jeans and a polo. Looking back, I was all over the map, and did not bring my "A" game.

At that time, I never wondered: who would give a professional that shows up in jeans and a polo any of their best connections? Or even better, some of those network events/meetings could have and do at times become a first-stage interview.

Back to your brand. *Who are you? How do you want to be known?* Then visualize that side of yourself and make sure you develop and present that person each time you walk out of the house and into your next network meeting. By my next meeting I was ready, and minimally I always wore a shirt, tie, and dress slacks, and times I was in a full suit. This was whom I wanted to be, and how I wanted to present to anyone I came in contact with. It showed I was ready to start today, that I am already dressing the part.

To be honest, I am sure that how you look is also a big part of the first impression of anyone on the receiving end of my introduction. Like interviewing, judgments are being made in those first few seconds—it's just the facts of life. You want to make sure you put your best foot and attitude forward. With my renewed focus, I was going to network like it may become a job interview, or at minimum, the first face-to-face meeting in a long connection.

• • •

TIPS AND STRATEGIES:

Network like it may become a job interview—
or it is at least the first time you're meeting with an important connection.

As an example, I was able to secure a meeting at a networking event with a local CEO. If I showed up in the jeans and polo shirt at the end-of-day Monday meeting, I may have received a 20-minute discussion with perhaps one or two connections. However, I showed up in a suit and had done my due diligence on both the company and the CEO. That network event turned into a five-hour discussion with creating a potential job that the CEO and I developed, as well as several high-level connections that eventually led to the landing.

• • •

TIPS AND STRATEGIES:

Dress Up, Show Up, and Never Give Up!

Making it a productive meeting started the night before, when I did my homework on each individual. Sitting down at my desk I would put each name and date on a 5 x 8 page in my memo book in the left-hand corner, and in the right-hand corner I noted the number of connections we had in common. Then I noted a few of the common connections I knew pretty well, which I used to start the conversation "So I see we are connected to quite a few people, how well do you know Sarah?" Additionally, I wrote down some notes to companies that I may have done business with in the past or perhaps they graduated from a college my kids go to now. Note some things to find common ground and to get them to start to talk.

• • •

TIPS AND STRATEGIES:

We live in a world where everyone talks—*but we do not listen very well.* If you can truly listen, take notes, and be generally interested in what the interviewers or people you are networking with are saying—you will beat out the competition.

I tried to manage the time in a 70/30 split, letting them speak 70 percent of the time. Get to know your new connection. An introduction will get you the meeting, but finding a way to truly connect takes listening and genuine interest.

The 30 percent was split into two categories: The "Tell me about yourself" question in which you respond with your short and concise Value Proposition Statement (referenced earlier in this book). The other 15 percent was my response to the question: "So how can I help you." When I was networking during my first career transition, I met Tony who told me not to be too vague but not too specific. I wondered, "What the heck does that even mean?" He responded, "What is your favorite baseball team?" I told him and he said, so you're a left-field player and you go speak with them knowing that they just signed a star for a multi-million multi-year contract. However, you were so focused on that position that you didn't notice there was a position opening in right field."

I took that advice back to my home office, and after a few hours I came up with my response.

"I have two primary focuses I am looking for. Ideally, I am looking for a C-level position at a $30-$300 million-dollar manufacturing/technology company."

This would generate a 5 percent response relative to whether the listener/networker knew someone who knew someone. However, these positions will rarely be posted, and my thought was that at any given time, two people are speaking about an opportunity like this. It was my goal to know one of those two individuals through networking more than my competition did—and I did.

My second area is broken out into three categories. I am seeking connections to CEOs and board members, private equity firms, and the bankers and CPAs for small-to-medium-size businesses. First, it was all people that would hire someone like me, either for President/COO or senior operations position within a struggling business. Second, you always wanted to clarify the small-to-medium size because your view of that description may be different from the listeners.

So here I have learned to not be too specific but not too general, and using this new approach, I was able to leave a high percentage of network meetings with three to five more really good connections.

Build Your Pipeline

What I mean by this title is: how are you filling your day and week as it relates to networking, contacts, and connections? In transition, this is one of the critical factors in getting people that speak of you, tell your story to others, and be your cheerleader when you are absent and there is a discussion of opportunities.

I have found success in first "singing on top of the mountain" your story to all; part of this process is a numbers game, so getting your name out there is essential. Truly knowing the ones that will hire your skillset, service, knowledge, etc. are the ones you should continue to target to meet.

• • •

TIPS AND STRATEGIES:

Enable your cheerleaders to speak for you, but let them know your message so they can introduce you to others that are in line with your target list.

For example, after a few months of my transition with me spreading my net wide so I can fill my pipeline (day/week), I put the "shotgun" approach on the shelf and picked up the "sniper" rifle.

My list consisted of the following:

- **Private Equity Firms**

I have found that getting into private equity is a pretty difficult process, especially if you do not have a background in private equity. It's a different world, and sometimes has higher standards from the financial-results side than large, publicly traded companies. Make sure your message is short, concise, and something that they are looking for. Private equity companies that either had newly purchased a company or had a market change within one of their existing companies, and now they need a subject-matter expert. Or the firm's profits are not going well, so perhaps they need a financial expert or operations specialist. Either way, you must prime the pump before you need the water—and you need an opportunity. Through networking again, reaching out with a Value

Proposition statement was one way I found to gain access to the decision-makers. I used:

> *"I'd like to introduce myself, George Murray, I am a military veteran and business executive with 18 years' experience in global operations. I position stagnant or declining companies to create a competitive advantage for Continuous Growth. Experienced in RFID (Embedded Technology), Automation, and Automotive industries."*

Forget your one-minute "Elevator Speech;" they don't have time. Private Equity likes people who are sure of themselves in their discipline and like to be bold. Words from a best-selling author Harvey MacKay are: "Dig your well before you're thirsty."

- **Company CEOs, Board Members, and Senior Vice Presidents**

PE firms' CEOs, and executives of companies, are very busy, however; the good ones I have found in transition are always looking for talent in both good and bad times. First identify the companies you're looking to network in or potential opportunities. Again, take your Value Proposition and tweak it to their current need/situation.

> —Their profitability is dropping on either flat or declining sales, and they will need someone who can come in and help in the short-term increase profitability, but also help either with strategy shift or tactical execution of that new strategy. Formulating your Value Proposition in the shortest message will let them know you are a subject-matter expert, and you took the time to research their company/situation, and then you close with your plan as if you were on their team (See 90-Day Plan).

- **Business Bankers and Business Attorneys**: Why? They tend to know when a business is in distress and needs leadership support or change even before the owner or executive leader does. They use data and numbers instead of oversight and feelings. Views and feelings can be clouded, misjudged, and all the while the company/organization continues to fall in a downward spiral.

Fill your pipeline for the days ahead once the responses come back from emails, LinkedIn connections, and warm introductions from other connections.

Uber Networkers

In any city/town/state there are what I call "Uber Networkers," people who for many reasons are very connected with a large network. If you do any amount of networking, these names will quickly come out in general discussion from many different people.

They're well connected not only because they realized the power of networking—or they have fallen into a transition and learned the hard way the value of networking. Either way, they have a vast network, and they also have great knowledge of what is working for those in transition, and what is not. Why? You may be in transition a few weeks or a few months, but they have been out there for years. They have seen what is working and not working, depending on your background; they have also seen the shifts in the market, for example there may be fewer sales people in transition, but more finance people.

These Uber Networkers have become urban economic marketing specialists. They see the shifts in the economy demand, and they also see the old trends and the new trends in networking. They are highly articulate in the ways of gaining leverage over your competition and in providing extremely valuable feedback. Seek out more of these Uber Networkers, and if you're able, make sure you have a few on your personal board of advisors, as they are ones that you continue to return to often that will help you keep your pipeline full both during and after your transition.

I found them a valuable resource on an ongoing basis. Every five to seven weeks in transition, you should be circling back around; not only to get reconnected but to also update them. They are networking with all sorts of people in transition, those just landed, or those looking to make adjustments to their staff, etc.

10-10-10

One way of doing this process I learned from a great friend and one of my early connections, He told me that I needed to fill my pipeline, and the best way to do so was the 10-10-10 principle: *10 emails/letters a day, 10 phone calls a day, and 10 face-to-face meetings a day.* WOW! Does that sound like a lot of work? That's your job to get a job so get to work. I was networking with two to three people a day, and maybe 10-15 a week. That was a big gap. Although I lived in Minnesota, I had been working in Wisconsin, so my name and experience hadn't had any exposure or network in Minnesota. Although this process was loosely outlined, I was able to perfect it, and really bring it to the next level.

The first 10 is Email/Letters. To find your content, get the local business section of a newspaper or business journal. Our local paper listed the "Movers/Shakers"—people that recently took a position that meets your criteria. You can get information from recently landed executives, professionals, etc. from all sorts of funnels. Recent newspapers, professional publications, plus local Chamber of Commerce are just a few avenues. Don't forget your local library. These old-school techniques are very rarely used now and can differentiate you from the mass.

Before you write, realize that most of these people are still new in their position, and busy, so make the letter short enough to respect their time but proposing your Value Proposition.

The letter should include:
- The first part should be congratulatory to them. My process was two to three lines acknowledging their recent success, transition, etc.
- The second paragraph should be your Value Proposition.
- Then the following was "who I am," again two to three sentences, with one line of what I used as "You Super Power, and how is it relevant to the reader." The sentence should resonate with them and put out the proverbial hook.
- Then ask if you can schedule a brief meeting, or minimally, a call so you can increase your networking.
- Finally, the ask—something along the lines of:

"I am looking forward to meeting with you for coffee and a face-to-face discussion to get some insight of the company culture as you see it (if the company is on your target list): ..." looking to meet and get some advice in small-to-medium-size industries, etc.

I would refrain from asking about a potential opportunity that is vacant. Let the face-to-face meeting bring that out in a non-direct way.

Here's how I did it from a time-management perspective:
√ Cold Calling – Know Your Message

I was highly skeptical of this approach—first the fear of what to say, and then the possible rejection. A friend and I were having a network catch-up meeting six months into my first transition when the topic came up. He asked me what was working and what was not working, sort of a self-reflection point in time. Then he asked me what I could do differently, which later helped me outline the "Stop/Start/Continue Model" (discussed earlier). I went off to the drawing board with a new potential approach.

On Tuesday evening, I sat there wondering whom I would reach out to, and what my message was going to be. While doing that, I was also following up on the network actions, and one was reaching out and following up on calls (see 10-10-10). I reached out to a connection at a major corporation, but because it was too late, he wasn't available. Then I thought perhaps a direct approach to the CEO as it was a company I was interested in, based on all I had researched: Culture, Leadership, Direction, Brand, etc. What message could I leave or ask a CEO of a major Fortune 500 company that would make him want to speak to me or respond to a message? It had to be impactful, short but enough to drive the message and the "ask."

Three hours later, I had outlined my message that was now ready to be sent to the CEO. To my surprise and unpreparedness, that CEO called me two days later. WOW! My five-minute discussion with him seemed much more, and the discussion was very memorable. He told me, "George, that was a powerful message, short and to the point, and interested me enough to reach back out to you. How long was that message?" "Sir, it was approximately 20 seconds," to which he responded "Impactful, use it often." I was able to speak with him a few more times, and he requested my resume and shared it with some other very influential leaders.

• • •

TIPS AND STRATEGIES:

Cold Calling still works: Know your message. Be Direct!

The message I left was:

Mr. CEO, this is George Murray, a recently transitioning operations executive that took a company from $100M to $180M in 18 months. I am looking to network in the medium-to-large business community and would love five minutes of your time for some insight.

My most recent position was a result of a direct message to the CEO. I did my research. It was a local opportunity; however, the company was publicly traded and its corporate operations were located in Massachusetts.

Using all the social media sites to see comments, news, and a market analysis, I created my "Value Proposition" introduction to the CEO through LinkedIn. You have limited characters to make the best first impression. It's not your elevator pitch, it's not a warm introduction (in this instance). You are interrupting their day, so it has to be impactful enough, and the added answer to "What can you do for me" must be more than another interruption.

Two days later I received a call from Massachusetts. The CEO started the conversation: "Thanks for reaching out. Our interviewing process has kicked off, and you will need to catch up and be flexible." Absolutely. In a few rounds and five weeks, I received an offer. And after the short negotiation, I happily took the offer which I started two weeks later.

• • •

TIPS AND STRATEGIES:

Be direct, do your homework, lead with your Value Proposition.

Networking Events – Tag-Team Introductions – Wingman/Wing Woman
Going to an event can be somewhat scary and overwhelming. Review the agenda, and knowing some of the major networkers can be an advantage. Even more of an advantage is going with a close connection, someone who can be your "Wingman/Woman," and can help introduce you, and vice versa.

Going in with a game plan is critical to ensure your event goes as well as you planned. Outline a critical 15–20 second introduction of each other, again outlining that Value Proposition and perhaps that "Super Power" each one of you has that generates the "Buzz," and open up the dialogue for each networker. I refer to "Super Power" as the one thing you are uniquely known for—and how you are able to gain the incredible success in the shortest amount of time.

When each one of you walks up to the group and there is a break in the conversation, the introduction is ready. "Jeff, I would like you to meet George Murray, he is a Rappel Master, he jumps into challenging situations like in his military days; he pulls the team together, sets a strategy and leads the team to success. Would you know anyone who needs someone like George?" Or how about "Jeff, meet George, he is a bit of a Pole Vaulter, he sets his teams and his goals high, like a Pole Vaulter's view above the bar to clear it; he and his team always meet and most of the time exceed budget goals. Would you know anyone who would need someone like George?"

Agreed, it's a play on words but it's more exciting than, "Meet George, a VP of X Company, blah, blah, blah."

You both should have a plan before you enter the network event. Don't try to get everyone's business cards. This will cheapen your brand—and you will not have time to truly connect with people. If you're able to obtain the attendee list ahead of time or get the names of some of the speakers or power-play individuals, take some time the night before to do your homework on them. This will be obvious when you do get a chance to introduce yourself, and the person will become more genuinely interested in the discussion.

If the event is a big one of 50 to 150-plus attending, and it's over an hour long, I would try to get three to five really valuable connections. This will give you the opportunity to follow up post-event, and the time you shared will be more memorable.

Remember to be respectful of the networkers' time as well, do not "hog" the entire discussion, and if you know others there, a great way to professionally excuse yourself and help others is to pull someone else into the conversation.

Keeping Top of Mind in Transition

Trying to stay top of mind with all the people you network with over time can be a challenge. It's not that they truly mean to forget you; time simply has a way of moving fast for them and perhaps slow for you. A great way to stay top of mind with your network is that every five to seven weeks give a brief update on your progress, no more than four to six lines, then another paragraph on specifically what you are looking for; either connections or your ideal position, or company.

• • •

TIPS AND STRATEGIES:

When in transition, update your network every five to seven weeks, and be sure to put everyone on Blind Copy (BCC) so they do not get "reply all" and feel they are on a mass distribution list.

That way both those you know and also the new people you network with know your status and what you have been up to. It's also a good way for them to give you a bit of an update if you ask toward the end of the email. Let's face it, when you start networking you will quickly realize that you are not the only one networking. Updating the people that you network with, and do it often, will keep you "top of mind" when they are networking with others, and if an opportunity gets discussed that requires your skillset or background, they will remember you and make the connection. One of those people may have recently spoken with someone that has an ideal position for you, but the person you networked with hasn't heard from you in over a month. "Hmm, Fred must have landed, I will suggest someone else"—or they may forget about you all together.

After you land your ideal position, I suggest using this format to keep your network updated while you are employed, doing so perhaps two to three times per year. Again, it keeps you top of mind, as well as being a great way to keep your network updated. We tend to fall into a "head-down, work" mentality and forget to continue networking. The next time you need it, you might have to start from scratch with those who haven't heard from you since your last transition three to four years ago. How willing do you think they will be to help you?

The following is an example of an update I used in August 2018:

I am blessed; in the past few months I have been able to meet many new as well as updated contacts. The list is quite large to identify everyone, however, Lisa XXX, Nicki XXX, Chris XXX, George XXX, Mark XXX, Julie XXX, Tony XXX, and many others have helped introduce me to even more connections. – Thank you all!!!

At Company X, I went to the final round, but they decided to go in a different direction due to restructuring of Company X. Bummer, due to the fact of my years' experience in "blank" manufacturing. XXX Manufacturing Company opportunity in Wisconsin doesn't seem to be optimal but I'd still like an opportunity with that manufacturing company. Great Company.

However, I am in second-round interviews with two different machine companies that will be multiple plant operations as VP Operations positions, a few more Private Equity firms looking for new President/CEO—due to my previous experience with PE firms (however would take me out of Minnesota). I just submitted to a water filtration company for the Operations Director position with HR. So things are progressing.

Again, things are progressing but I'm getting stir crazy to get back to work.

I am working two paths to my next position:

1. *COO/President of a $150M or less, Manufacturing/Technology company, ideally.*
2. *Senior Director/VP of a large OEM (List specific companies you are interested in) activity due to many factors such as little succession planning, etc. Companies with a weak bench strength may be looking for my skill/background.*

Would love to get an update from you. If there is something that I can do for you or help you connect to someone, please contact me.

Vision Boards

A good friend I met while in transition told me about Vision Boards. *Thank you, Jenny.* It's a tool that helps one get more focused, concentrate better, and identify what is important. People do these boards at all times in their life—whether it's a young professional starting to identify goals and life aspirations, or someone who wants to shift gears in life or as a midlife-crisis exercise.

I found during transition it helped me to stay motivated, with pictures of a healthy life, food, exercise, etc. You can add on the family, whether it's a picture of the ideal family vacation, or just spending more time, with words in bold. Add the specific jobs or careers with either word and/or pictures. Place it in an area that you will see more than a few times in a day to help keep you focused and inspired to work toward your goal.

Your visual boards can change as many times as you delete or add more items, depending on your achievements or shift in focus. This tool is meant to pull your creative side along with your strategic side of your life, family, career, etc. The size of the board is up to the individual, and the more I research it and ask others, the size has no limits. It's what motivates you, not others, your family, etc.

Energy, Enthusiasm, and a Positive Attitude

• • •

TIPS AND STRATEGIES:

It goes without saying that during networking or interviewing, you have to bring controlled (not over-the-top) Energy, Enthusiasm, and a Positive Attitude.

Being well-rested is critical to ensure you bring a level of energy so that other people can feel the energy themselves in a positive way, and find they are drawn to you. Showing just enough enthusiasm to the person or interviewer feels that you respect their time and generally you are interested in what they have to say.

Finally, a positive attitude is key as no one wants to work with an individual who seems to emit, "Oh, woe is me…" If you do not bring these three things: Energy, Enthusiasm, and a Positive Attitude, you may want to reschedule or call in sick. Your brand is tested each time you put yourself out there, and you don't want to tarnish it by having a bad day.

Personal Board of Advisors

We all need help from time to time, but whether we chose to ask for it or accept it is another story altogether. I found building a personal board of advisors was critical to my career transition success. I had never experienced this before: what should I do, not do, how do I cope, etc.

I was in career transition when I read *True North* by Bill George, previous CEO of Medtronic; he wrote on the best practices of many leaders, including a "Personal Board of Advisors." These are three to five people that are from different backgrounds with common goals that can help you, guide you, introduce you, and listen to you. The book's one example shows his board of advisors informing him not to take one opportunity he might have regretted taking later.

They are professionals that you can heavily rely on to give you honest feedback:

- LinkedIn Expert – Help me "Get noticed" and ensure I had all the right keywords, etc.
- Friend – Not just any friend, one who could hold me accountable, listen, advise, support, etc.
- Financial Advisor – Ensure my expenses didn't run away, offer alternatives, etc.
- Energy Coach – Someone who can bring you up when you're down, a positive person who can help you from a different perspective.
- Working Peer – Someone that can help you find new opportunities, bounce ideas off of, and help you connect to the working network.
- "Mirror" people – those who will give you the truth, holding up that mirror. They provide honest and constructive feedback to questions you pose.

I spoke to some "advisors" every day or every other day; others were weekly or monthly. You also need to ask if they will support you in that function because when you get that "Thank you for applying, but we went in a different direction" response on Friday and need to talk, most people are off till Monday. However, if you have a personal board of advisors, they are there for you.

As you grow personally and professionally, your board members may change, and you may add new board members. To progress you must always surround yourself with people that will challenge you. What if you had the Board of Advisors of Elon Musk, Martin Luther King, Nelson Mandela, John F. Kennedy, Tony Robbins, and Simon Sinek (yes, some have passed), what could you be capable of doing?

● ● ●

TIPS AND STRATEGIES:

How motivated would you be if you had a personal board of advisors that speak about your skills with such passion, determination, and inspiration.

If you are already in a career, still create your own to help you be more successful.

CHAPTER 5
The How-To to Land Your Next Position

TIPS AND STRATEGIES:

The Value Proposition should put you at the top of the pile to advance you to the next face-to-face round.

Increase Your Odds to Start the Interview Process

To increase your chances through each step of the interview process, the three parts are:

1. Phone screen call
2. Face-to-face interviews
3. Final-round interview

To be more successful than the average person in landing in their next position, you need to do more than the rest. There is a process that you can follow to increase your chance for success through each round.

A low percentage of job opportunities are found by submitting a resume directly to a company. Websites like Indeed, Monster, CareerBuilder, and other job sites have an easy way to ensure that the jobs come to you by outlining job-search criteria. They can send you emails daily, weekly, or whatever frequency so that you're not spending so much time searching it yourself.

Considerably more success in finding these opportunities is through your network. There is a right way and a wrong way to network for your next opportunity. Do your research before you unintentionally ruin your chances related to your future position.

Throughout the interview process, continue to research and network within the company. Yes, this will separate you from the majority of the competition in the interviewing process.

The Phone Screen Call

You need to make sure that you prepare for the initial phone screen call. You would think most people would do this; however, most don't do an in-depth background check on the company in order to articulate the reasons you've selected the opportunity—and what you could bring to the potential position. If you thoroughly do your homework, you can have excellent dialogue and a higher chance of moving on to the next round.

Additionally, what people do not take into account is dressing up to look your best for a phone screen. Yes, you read that right, dressing up for a phone screen interview. I found in my military days that when you dressed up, you stood straighter, spoke with more confidence, and came across more positive—which the interviewer will be able to feel. *Those you are talking to will notice the difference.*

Finally, it's essential that you genuinely listen to the person on the other end. All too often the feedback that I received from talking with other hiring managers was that they were continuously interrupted mid-sentence. The phone screen call is to see if you fit the essential requirements and meet the cultural criteria. If you were interviewing for a leadership position, as an example, leaders must understand and listen to the situation before asking questions or making decisions.

To respond clearly and concisely based on the questions you're asked, you should follow the SAR response process:

- S – Situation: When they ask you a question, like: "Tell me a time _____," you should briefly outline the situation before you respond.
- A – Action: What action did you specifically take to get the results? For example, I did X, Y and Z.
- R – Results: Finally, you finish with the results. This can be another two to four sentences, based on real data.

For example, the question could be: Tell me a time when you took significant action to improve the overall business. For example, I could say: When I entered the operation, the on-time delivery was struggling to achieve greater than 70 percent consistently, and I pulled the team together and reviewed the data. We were able to create a cause-and-effect diagram based on all the issues that caused the on-time delivery to achieve 98 percent or better. I split the team into three groups, and we started to work on the top three issues. In 12 weeks, we achieved the first 98 percent on-time delivery and consistently sustained 98 percent.

Once the interviewer/employer completes their questions, you can start to clearly and concisely respond or ask more in-depth questions.

At this stage, it is crucial that you have only one to three specific questions. The screening call ensures that you meet the educational qualifications, reinforces you are within the budgetary range for the position, and could be a cultural fit. These questions should be formulated based on the homework that you have done on the company. One of the last items I ask is "When you have hired the ideal candidate, and are doing the first-year review, what successes will that person achieve." The response to this question will enable you to follow up with a Value Proposition "one-pager" that we will go over later.

The Face-to-Face Interview

It's no surprise that first impressions are always important. The difference is that this time it will be face-to-face—and in general, opinions are formed in less than 20 seconds.

If you are of the age where you think that age discrimination may be a factor, you need to take a close look in the mirror. Yes, seriously, I know we can't drop 20 pounds overnight, but we can make sure that we are well-groomed, and the clothes that we select will have a good fit and professional look.

Additionally, if your hairstyle hasn't changed in the last 10 to 15 years, it may be an excellent time to get an updated look; however, don't go too extreme. For example, I decided to cut my hair shorter, and that in itself made me look a few years younger and gave me a little more self-confidence. Other things to consider: maybe if you wore a beard or started to turn gray, you may want to shave the beard or use a product to chase away the gray. These things are tough to tell people; however, the ones who listened and applied the insight, secured better odds in the interview.

After you've taken a good, honest look in the mirror and feel sure you're ready to be received well, you need to prepare to go into more depth about your background. The knowledge comes from not only the phone screen but also your additional homework on the company, and where you may be able to add value.

Remember These Three Things:
1. Smile. Most interviewees tend to get so wrapped up in their message that they forget to smile and remain positive.
2. Breathe and remain calm. Interviewing is stressful, and whether you are talking to a panel or the hiring manager, make sure you stay on point.
3. Listen to the question from the interviewer. Often the interviewer asks a question, and the interviewee goes off on a tangent, never answering the original question. At times it may be most beneficial to ask a clarifying question before you answer the original question, which enables you to show the interviewer that you were listening. Only use this technique sparingly.

Listening will enable you to reinforce the questions that you received answers to on your phone screen call with the people that are interviewing you. Additionally, it will also strengthen your ability to leave them with the second "Wow," which is the Value Proposition. (See below)

One of the tasks that you need to be working on for your face-to-face interview is taking the answers from the questions that you have and formulate your own one-page Value Proposition for both the HR manager and the hiring manager that includes:

- Three to five things that they identified in the phone screen call that are crucial for this position, listing them on the left-hand column in an Excel spreadsheet, and then two columns to the right. The first column should outline the three to five things that the company identified as crucial for this

position in the next 6-12 months. Put this in an Excel format to the left column.
- The middle column is the actions and situations in which you've been able to do what you have done to overcome similar obstacles in previous positions. This can reinforce your skills, abilities and past performance can help them in their current challenges.
- Third column lists the results that you achieved.

Then edit and place it in a Word document that fits on one page. See the example below. You will want to leave this with the hiring manager and HR manager after you've had your face-to-face interview—the first stage of giving them a "Wow," in a more tangible way with the document. Again, what you are trying to do is separate yourself from the remaining candidates. When they review all candidates, they will have resumes in one pile—and in the other pile is your Value Proposition statement and your 90-day plan (which we will outline later in the hiring process).

The Value Proposition

• Contact me to create your own Value Proposition •
georgecmurray@gmail.com

George C. Murray, MBA
georgecmurray@gmail.com | www.linkedin.com/in/georgecmurray

COMPETENCIES	EXPERIENCE	ACCOMPLISHMENTS
Building a Culture of Inclusion	• Employee engagement and retention • Learning & development • Performance management • Flexible work arrangement	• Open, effective communication, as well as clear channels for feedback • Educational Approach Developed several low cost programs that increased communication, effectiveness, and feedback (same page) across 3 continents Developed One on One Mentoring/Coaching sessions for next generational leaders
Developing and execute an account level strategy across all relationship managers	• Better understanding the business opportunity embedded in the client base • Execute with accountability • Create client experience that strengthen client loyalty • Create a strategic business partner relationship	• Better understanding existing clients • Higher level of client satisfaction • Long term revenue and asset growth Led and managed Turnaround in Chrysler Account; Developed strategic plan to improve Toro relationship and customer service level from 58% to over 99% within 4 months sustaining
Hiring and assessing talent	• Hire high performers from the market leader • Develop a hiring profile to structure and standardize the process for improved results • Elevate the role and expectations of the relationship manager	• Build bench strength • Higher client satisfaction and loyalty scores • Better client retention and market share • Outperform revenue objectives Developed and refined a candidate profile which was deployed globally
Industry Sales Leadership	with Fortune 500 companies & small/medium level companies • Contribute sales leadership; identify and develop key opportunities for improvement • Bring market leadership perspective to the sales leadership group • Bringing state of the art compensation practice for relationship managers and sales representatives	• Knowledge and experience from market leader • Tapping into best practices • Understanding of high level client satisfaction and loyalty • Attracting and retaining top talent • Assurance that compensation practices meet standards Led a cross functional team to develop a 3 years sales strategy that would grow the company by 250%
Experience/knowledge of industry and trends	• Provide thought leadership to the process of moving from where you are to where you want to be as the market changes	• Prepare for future success • Respond to changing market trends • Be a valued resource to target clients • Outlined Supplier Day and Customer Day that created Brand awareness and further sales of 15%
Executive level capabilities	• Ability to participate in strategic initiatives and groups • Bring a strong voice of client expectations • C-Suite access and strategic dialogue	• As the industry changes we can respond to changing trends and competitions Led a series of C-level roundtables on Industry trends
Sales opportunities–know the firms to go after	• Create an enterprise initiative to recruit target prospects and clients	• Increase market share • Disruption of the competition Defined the break-away automotive & branding market and executed a business plan which produced $41 million growth in sales Outlined Sales & Business Growth Strategy for a Contract Capital Equipment Manufacturing Company for 3 year plan to grow from $18M–$36M.
Continuous Improvement Driver	• Create low cost visual managements system that formulized a set of mission-driven key success measures • Develop technology infrastructure to support real time data for better & quicker business decisions • Increase employee engagement which drive efficiency and reduced direct labor costs	• Aligned continuous improvement with strategic objectives • Integrate continuous improvement into a culture of strategic execution • Blend the best practices from the different methodologies and international cultures • Focus on data, not emotions Identified and led a $4.1 million hard savings initiative across multiple global factories in first year Drove $1.7M overhead cost reduction through machine automation throughout the organization

The Second Face-to-face/Team Interview

Congratulations, you have already beaten out 85 percent of the applicants. But what you need to do now is reinforce your skills and abilities, and ensure that you can align with the culture that's within the organization.

You should be networking within the organization to get an insightful understanding of the culture—i.e., understand the leadership, how people solve problems, and how they collaborate. Connect to personnel that are within the company through LinkedIn or get introduced by other mutual connections to increase your chances during the process. This would give you another advantage as you may be going up against anywhere from four to seven other applicants.

Another preparation is making sure that you have more in-depth questions for this particular round than for your phone screen call. You could outline one-to-two dozen specific questions that relate to all aspects of the job description and the area you will be responsible for, and ask two to three of those questions to the interviewee related to their background. For example, a financial interviewer asks questions related to what they would be able to answer like, "Tell me the challenges with the increase in inventory—and what has the team identified?"

The power suit for either male or female—it's crucial to dress in something that's both professional, and something that makes you feel like you can take on the world. You may also want to add an accent like a color tie that matches your eyes. Something I wear on my suit is my army label pin, which each veteran gets when they leave the military. This small accent can generate a great conversation and get them to learn about you more on a personal level.

You're ready for your face-to-face interview. Make certain that you know the route in case you have to take an alternate route as things happen in life. Also leave one and a half times earlier than what the direction instructs so that you can prepare for any obstacles and still make it there on time.

Don't forget to bring a notebook with 1) the questions, 2) your Value Proposition statement, and 3) some examples of your work so that you may be able to tell a story and show results. Also remember to breathe, listen, lean in toward the interviewer, and smile. Let the interviewer finish the question before starting to answer it.

Again, body language is highly visible during the first meeting. It's essential that you smile, have a firm handshake, good eye contact, and also show enthusiasm, a positive attitude, and a level of energy.

Once you finished with each interviewer, it's essential to thank them for their time, smile and ask them for the next steps in the process because you are still interested in the opportunity. Many people forget that stage, and it leaves the company questioning whether or not the interviewee is still interested. Do not leave any doubt.

Make sure that you leave your Value Proposition for the HR manager and hiring manager. Also write a follow up with a "Thank you note" to each individual person for their time, explanation of the opportunity, and a personal response based upon the face-to-face meeting that you had. One example can be a more in-depth response to a specific question that they deemed critical for this position.

In closing, make sure you get business cards/contacts of all the people you interviewed. This will enable you to send "Thank you" notes to each and ensure you clearly articulate something related to the specific interview. This will give you the ability to further answer a specific question and shows you listen, take notes, and follow up. Make sure you do this within 24 hours. Handwritten "Thank you" notes are an added plus and if you bring them with you, you can fill them out in the parking lot after the interview while it's all fresh in your mind.

Always leave them with a WOW!

Final-Round Interview

At this point, anywhere from two to four people are seriously considering the same opportunity. You will have to up your game a bit more to separate yourself from the "Thank you for your time, but we decided to go with another candidate" to "Congratulations, we want to make you an offer."

You can separate yourself in a few ways from the rest of the candidates at this interview level. You can create a presentation relative to the position that you were applying for. In it outline the markets, business opportunities, or overall improvements that you may be able to suggest and execute in your first six months to a year that aligns with the hiring manager's requirements.

Additionally, you may want to rehearse your points so that you are not speaking to the PowerPoint slides, but you are telling a story, and the slides are going to reinforce the details of the story that you're communicating.

90-Day Plan

Another opportunity to separate yourself from the few remaining candidates is creating a 90-Day Plan based on all the discussions going back to the initial phone screen to the final face-to-face conversations. Although many companies like to tout their onboarding process, very few companies outline a plan to get a professional or executive up to speed in the shortest amount of time. The 90-Day Plan helps you create an outline for you and the hiring manager on the critical tasks to be accomplished in the first 90 days. You can also use it as a weekly check-in to ensure you and the hiring manager are in alignment with the progress.

The 90-Day Plan can outline your industry knowledge as well as the changes in people, departments, and processes that you will take in your first 90 days to come up to speed on the critical topics. These points are a little more than just general statements, and reinforce the information you received in the previous interviews. The 90-Day Plan is an accumulation of all of the one-on-one, face-to-face, and phone screen calls that outline the job, the challenges, etc., and your approach to hit the ground running. Provide one copy to the hiring manager, and one copy to the HR manager. You can do it in two ways, and based on your comfort level with the interviewing process, one way is to present it to them in the final-round process. Another is to send them in an email within 24 hours of the face-to-face last-round interview.

Need help with creating your 90-Day Plan,
Contact me: georgecmurray@gmail.com

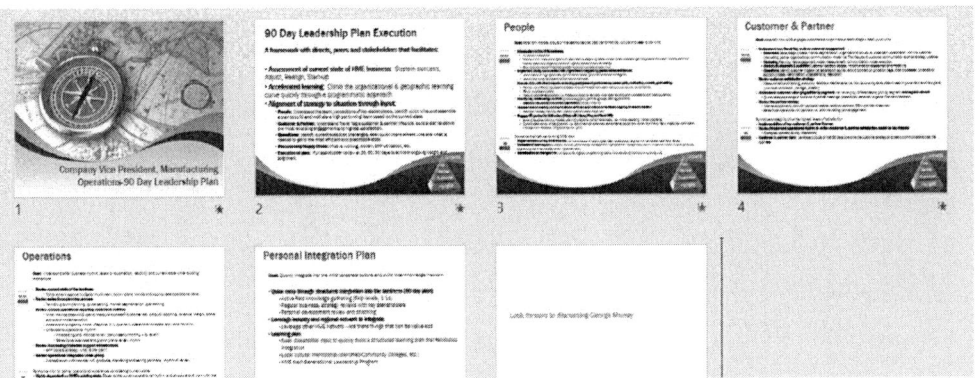

Always follow up with a thank you for the time they spent with you, and also articulate two to three key takeaways from the interview, reinforcing your skills and abilities.

The overview of this entire process is that as they start to interview, the stack of resumes dwindles to the final few. Most people don't realize that there is another stack. Very few people add anything to that important stack at each phase of the interviewing process. Vital information is given in the Value Proposition, the presentation or 90-Day Plan, and always the thank you note. Following these processes will make you stand out, better your chances, and land a new position over your competition.

• • •

TIPS AND STRATEGIES:

After the initial interviews, giving a potential employer a 90-day plan for what you would do at his company will put you at the head of the line.

Although highly recommended and written about in many articles, few people put in the work needed to complete this for a potential employer. By doing this, you have already put yourself at the head of the pack. As you listen to the phone screen and the face-to-face interviews, you will uncover focus points and also obstacles, and you should be putting a plan in place to address those, along with being able to create bridges and alliances with the new potential colleagues.

Your deep and intriguing questions will not only give you a better understanding of the landscape, it will also give the interviewer your truly deep interest in the job. You now have enough to establish a framework or department that you will "touch" in the first 30 days. Both employees and employers like leaders that are actively engaged and out of their offices so they can hear and see the challenges that were expressed in the interviewing process.

The 90-day plan covers *People, Processes, and Challenges* of the position for which you are interviewing. Sitting with key talent and asking them basic open-ended questions will help you put together a 90-Day plan for you to review in your final round with both the hiring manager and human resources. However, you have to outline what that first 90 days would look like, and this should be the major differentiator that has them select you over the competition. Most people are only following up, perhaps sending the "Thank you, why you should hire me" note; however, few are leaving them with the "Wow" and the "How I would outline my first 90 days if you decide on me." Further reinforcing that "We can modify this the first week during my onboarding." We know they already expect you to know your role—really, how many executives/professionals get a proper onboarding? Now you have already outlined it for them.

When I sat down with my previous bosses at my last three positions, I asked them what was the one thing that made it easier for them to choose me. Answer was "Your 90-Day plan." It was a differentiator, and no one else had previously presented information to them in that way.

Continually evaluating your progress will enable you to brainstorm and try new things. I had to:

- Continue to do the things I felt were working for me.
- Keep networking. By far networking was something I was going to continue and get better at, trying to ensure I could get more quality connections that could impact my steps closer to my next opportunity.
- Stop anything that was not working for me; whether that might be sending out letters, cold calling, etc.
- Finally, spend some time on things that I might start to do or try again, like cold calling, sending direct impactful LinkedIn invites to people whom would hire the position or people that work at companies I might be interested in. By the way, I received an 85 percent response rate to those invites. Remember your message has to be impactful because you have only 300 characters to make a first great impression.

One example of my introduction through LinkedIn is as follows: below used before

> *I'd like to introduce myself, George Murray, a military veteran, and business executive with 18 years' experience in global operations. I position stagnant or declining companies to be competitive again. I also coach and mentor as well as speak on Career Transition, Supervisor, and Day in the Life for better success.*

Again, you have less than 30 seconds or a few lines to make a great first impression, so make the most of it. This was a great practice to keep your creative juices flowing, and to wake you up to some things that str just not working for you—and you are just aimlessly going through the daily steps.

Follow-up Email

Even with all the articles and recommendations on sending a follow up, so many people still skip this critical last attempt to plug your skills and keep your name relevant and top of mind. During all your face-to-face interviews, collect business contacts and key takes away with each person so you can make sure that your email can contain part of either the questions you were able to answer or a topic you can clarify further.

Be sure you keep the email as positive as possible, highlighting your strengths related to the challenges they are currently experiencing. I found that filling in their gaps complements your skills and reinforces the need for them to select you over the competition.

Questions
1. What are the biggest challenges that someone in this position would face?
2. What training programs are available to your employees?
3. What will you expect from me during the first 90 days, six months, and first year of employment?
4. What gets you most excited about this company's future?
5. Can you tell me about my direct reports? What are their strengths and the team's biggest challenges?
6. Can you tell me about the last team (or office) event you did together?
7. What are the next steps in the selection process?

CHAPTER 6
Your "Job," While Looking for a Job

Learning Experience:
Vacations, Time off, etc.

Prior to my first job transition, I had saved up close to 800,000 air miles, and not having a vacation with just my wife while the kids were growing up, I planned our first vacation for the two of us in over 20 years. Just three weeks before we were to take our vacation, I was laid off. The air miles I saved up took 755,000 of those miles just to cover the flight. We had prepaid about 70 percent of the vacation for ten days in Bora Bora. Even with all my international travel, my wife had never been outside of the United States, because the kids took precedence.

My wife wanted us not to go, saying "We can't afford to go." I said, "We already paid for 70 percent of it and we will lose it all. We can't afford *not to go*." With great hesitation on my wife's part, we went anyway, not knowing what the future career held. Long story short, it was the greatest place I had ever seen, and I had seen a lot of places in my time. It was the only time I didn't have a phone or computer attached to me. It took me three days, but finally this strange feeling came over me while sitting on the beach with my wife drinking one of those umbrella fruity drinks—*it was the first time I had become calm, focused, and relaxed.*

At that point I didn't know it would take me another six months before I would land a new opportunity. Moral of this point: Take the vacation! You worked very hard, and if you're anything like me, likely you're wound tighter than a snare drum. Your body, mind, and family demand that you take it. It's critical for your mental health and your relationship because at the end of every day, you leave the job—and the family is always there waiting.

• • •

TIPS AND STRATEGIES:

During your time in transition, schedule downtime from the hectic pace and stress of networking, interviewing, and job submission.

You can schedule three-day weekends, or schedule some specific time with the family on those weekends. This time is very stressful, and you are worrying 1000 percent of the time, so it's critical to take a break even if it's for a day. Maybe go to a movie. You are teaching your kids your resilience, and you're taking the much-needed time with them that you didn't when you were in your career.

Volunteering

You have the time now, why not volunteer, even for one day a week or month. It will get you out of the house and interacting with other people you wouldn't normally network or meet. You are giving to others that are less fortunate than you, and that's the best feeling. Meals on Wheels, your church, soup kitchens, and Feed My Starving Children are just a few volunteering places where you can sign up and walk right in and give a hand and your time. Volunteering and giving truly can help to put things into perspective, and *you'll feel grateful for what you have instead of what you don't.*

It also can be another avenue to network with others and share your Value Proposition, and your next opportunity can be a helping hand away. People want to help people who help people. Giving your time is much more than money, and you could make a difference in someone's day/week/month or even year. Results: you get more out of what you put into volunteering.

At my first few network meetings I met with a man (the second person I ever networked with in my first transition) who told me: "Life is short, and at the end of your life you have things (aside from your family that you love and love you) you can't take with you, so you should give away so others can benefit. Share both." *Thank you, Greg.*

Transition Life

Most executives and professionals are in their mid-life the first time they experience transition— and they have no clear path or plan. You would think with our diverse experiences we would know how to go about the transition. Unfortunately, like balancing a checkbook and creating a resume, the first time for young professionals is when they are transitioning into the workforce after graduating from school. They had not been taught those basics; however, neither is career transition taught to us.

That's the main reason why I wrote this book. At times it's far too late (or challenging) to learn a painful and lengthy process. Most of us are a sole breadwinner or the majority breadwinner, and when that funnel of income is abruptly broken, fear, frustration, etc. flood our small pool very fast. I wanted to provide a quick resource guide that if you were let go, left, etc. on a Monday, you could read this book in two days and be able to start a plan and process by Wednesday afternoon. It takes all the mistakes and delays from what I learned and puts them into a pretty clear process to follow for you to potentially cut your time in half.

• • •

TIPS AND STRATEGIES:

Transition life itself is a flood of emotions and sometimes all in one day: Hope, depression, focus, fog, frustration, elation, second-guessing, pride, and on and on.

That is why in transition I created the "Day in the Life." It was to help create structure in the most unstructured time in your life. *If you don't have a process, it is difficult to know what is going well and what is not working.* However, once you have a process and structure, you're able to evaluate each part of that process and adjust and use the continuous improvement mindset. Constantly evaluate with some timeframe. Certainly, not every day but at least every few weeks, use the: Start/Stop/Continue model. Start something new like explained in the book, *Cold Calling*—just make sure your message is clear and concise. Stop things that may not be working; perhaps networking with a certain level or certain industry (the industry might not be expanding). Finally, continue those things that are working, for example, networking events that are generating good leads and learning.

Another important part of the transition is the relationship (if you're married or in a long-term relationship)—is spending quality time together, but don't get down on each other. This is much easier said than done. Also don't rant on something that isn't going right because your significant other is already under a great deal of pressure, concern, and fear. It's good; however, to talk it out so you both are still on the same page and are able to talk positively to each other. For me, I couldn't have survived two transitions in two years without the discipline of how my wife Kerry managed the household money. I can't even imagine the worry she had 24/7 while I went out each day for "coffee meetings."

She often mentioned "What is this networking?" and "These coffee meetings are not getting you a job".... I tried to communicate the necessity to do both while trying to be most positive in a not-so-positive situation. It's important for both their understanding and your relationship to remain calm and articulate, explaining that gone are the days when you could just submit a resume and wait for them to call you. Your family is experiencing the same transition, and can feel more in the dark unless you keep them informed of both the progress and the challenges (without coming across as a victim).

You're lucky if you have a spouse or significant other, and this is important so you are not going it alone. They can also help cheer you up when days do not seem so positive or progressive. They can also be your amplifier, telling those she/he knows about your experience and capabilities while they are out in their day. It wouldn't be the first time that the next job/career opportunity was secured by someone's significant other.

Three things are important in career transition: being a student, a better listener, and helping others when you can. Be a student, which means to learn as much as you can. Learn about yourself, others, while in the process. Reading Stephen Covey's *7 Habits of Successful People:*

Sharpen the Saw, I learned so much it could be close to a degree in Humanities. Things to do, things not to do, and a lot about yourself you think you should know but life goes fast, and we always seem to be looking forward and focused on the outside for the most part. Perhaps career transition is a way for God to tell us to slow down, focus on what is important, and learn the lesson, #GetBetter.

• • •

TIPS AND STRATEGIES:

Life moves fast, and if we stop learning and stop listening, we truly become lost.

I found by listening to others that they become more interested in me. The world isn't educating us to listen. Listening has been around as long as we've had ears. However, we are using them less these days. Try this, go to your spouse or significant other and just listen, take notes (on pen and paper). This is intense listening, I bet if you do it for a month, your relationship will improve tenfold.

Finally, help others. Everyone can use help. As discussed, either volunteer, help others network, or help family and friends. Helping others give you a sense of accomplishment, sense of worth, and sense of pride, and those can be just as great as a monetary value. We all could use help, but we tend to forget the human spirit is to help—we just need to be clear what that help is. Be crystal clear. When helping others, ask them specifically: what can I do for you? You will be surprised the light you can bring into some person's gloomy day.

#GetBetter – Why?

I have referenced #GetBetter in this book a few times, and if you follow me on Instagram or LinkedIn, I use it a lot in my posts. Transition forced me and inspired me to #GetBetter. It's not meant to get better than someone else, just get better than who you were yesterday. Life will kick you, push you, and hit you hard, sometimes harder than you ever have been hit. A few times it might even continue to hit you hard time and time again. It's up to you to either lie on your back, curl up and give up—or look at your situation and say, "Hey, I am at the lowest point but I can see up, and if I can see up, I can get up and dust myself off."

I can then evaluate my situation, develop a plan, and then set a course. Perhaps it's my military training that developed my way of thinking.

• • •

TIPS AND STRATEGIES:

Even at your darkest days you can chose to lean forward and smile.

COVID-19

As I finish this book, we are experiencing COVID-19. Networking and productivity, like jobs, etc. took a nose dive. We were forced to self-quarantine and social distance, which became incredibly difficult for both networking, and since we are a social creature, we searched for how we could stay connected and move forward.

Weeks went by and we slowly came out of our caves through via Zoom, Virtual Networking, and Facetime, to name a few. What we didn't realize is if we were in career transition sitting at home, professionals and CEOs and other people were working from home. Their work hours were extended and their social society took the same nose dive. It goes back to earlier in the book where you had to find a way to reach out, cold call, cold email introduction, etc.

In reaching out, do not start off with "about you," but ask how they are doing. Be genuinely interested in where they are in their world. Lend an ear, find a way to be helpful even if it's just setting up time to talk. Take six to eight weeks to have two to three virtual discussions and again implement the 70/30-time usage; meaning let them talk 70 percent of the time.

This will create the true connection, and those people will remember you when all others went silent. Then slowly start switching the conversation more 50-50 percent. Discuss the challenges you have and ask for their insight. This is starting to create a relationship (higher level of networking). Over a few months you can create a lot of "cheerleaders," so when they are talking among other people and a job search comes up where your skills are required, you are the first they think of.

• • •

TIPS AND STRATEGIES:

Again, the basic concepts apply, but when you truly are interested in others, it will show, and those people will become your advisors and you can create followers that want to help you be more successful.

Finally ...
When you land, and you will, following your own "Day in the Life" process and tools, above all do not forget to stay networked. Find time to network with two or three new professionals a week either early for coffee before work, during a lunch, or after work just before going home

for dinner. Additionally, two to three times per year (again don't forget to blind copy them all so they do not feel they are on a spam email).

Closing

I consider this book the "best practice" of all the things I observed during both transitions. I wrote it to help those in transition outline a strategy sooner rather than later, and thus save time and wasted effort. If I knew half of this in the first month of my transition, I would have landed in half the time. A transition can be a good time or a bad time for you—either way without a plan, your time can go on and on with no clear end in sight. I met more than 1100 professionals and executives in transition (446 in my first and over 724 in my second). Many gave me both valuable information as well as great contacts. A few introduced me to my next opportunity, while they all taught me things that I hadn't learned yet.

They all gave me valuable time, which was worth much more than money. Do not ever discount an opportunity to give back. When someone gives their time, they are giving a very valuable commodity. Be thankful. Give back.

CHAPTER 7
Roadmap to a Successful Transition

Job transition can be a challenging journey—the following are the highlights (or milestones) of success:

CHAPTER 1:
Shock and Awe: Planning for the Next Rung to Grab Onto
- Always work hard to maintain a positive attitude, be enthusiastic, and exude high energy—because no one wants to talk to someone who isn't.
- To look for a job while in transition is the hardest job. There is no immediate monetary reward for all the efforts you put in. All the while you must maintain *a first great impression*.
- You might find that your life will change for the better. Mine did, once I focused on *what I had rather than what I didn't have.*

- Look at yourself in the mirror. Take a real close look. When I lost my job, I had to be brutally honest with myself for the first time in decades—and I made much-needed changes.
- If you do not take the time to honestly reflect and come to terms with *why you are at this stage in your life*, your next steps will be much more difficult, and you will continue to struggle.

CHAPTER 2:
The Much-Needed Tools for Success

- Based on my experience, most of your traffic will come from LinkedIn, so you will need to make sure your LinkedIn profile is optimized.
- Network tools for success—Business cards, network card, Value Proposition, and templates—are all tools to help you be more competitive and to save time.
- Prepare for the long haul and control what you can. The more senior your role had been, the longer it may be to find you next opportunity because of fewer jobs and more competition. Learn *what you can control, and what you can't.*

CHAPTER 3:
Be the Boss of YOU: Create Your Routine, Your "Day in the Life"—and Live It

- Lack of adequate sleep can affect many things in your life—energy throughout the day, memory, health, patience level, attitude about the world, and how you feel about yourself, just to name a few. Find ways that allow you *to get more essential hours of sleep.*

- Living in a very visual world, and with first impressions being made in less than seven seconds, which does not leave much time to say anything—you have to *always show up and be your best self.*
- Whether you work out, run or stretch, you can use the effective music to start your day and to put you in the right frame of mind.
- Continue using affirmations beyond your transition; change them up as necessary to keep you motivated and have an edge.
- Whoever you share your life with—it's important to increase your daily communication. Now is when you need to talk things through…together, and agree upon solutions.
- Kids are smart, smarter than you think, and treating them with respect, and letting them know what is going on, is a learning and teaching opportunity.
- We could all use better listening skills, especially if you're looking for a new leadership role.
- Be a student, a life-long learner during your transition time—and then continue learning all kinds of new things for the rest of your life.
- Each day on YouTube I had a different focus, and it was like a personal coach who I was able to get for free.
- Do not fail: Every three to four weeks, you must evaluate your progress.
- Everyone has life experiences that can resonate with others. Your path and the way you have overcome obstacles can be a lesson for someone else.

CHAPTER 4:
Be Prepared: Every Networking Opportunity Counts

- Once you give first or give often—people are more in favor of helping you later. *When I realized it's not all about me, I became happier, I became more connected, and I became more sought-out.*
- Network like it may become a job interview—or it is at least the first time you're meeting with an important connection.
- Dress Up, Show Up, and Never Give Up!
- Enable your cheerleaders to speak for you, but let them know your message so they can introduce you to others that are in line with your target list.
- Cold Calling still works: Know your message. Be Direct!
- Be direct, do your homework, lead with your Value Proposition.
- When in transition, update your network every five to seven weeks, and be sure to put everyone on Blind Copy (BCC) so they do not get "reply all" and feel they are on a mass distribution list.
- It goes without saying that during networking or interviewing, you have to bring controlled (not over-the-top) Energy, Enthusiasm, and a Positive Attitude.
- You would be much more motivated if you had a personal board of advisors that speak about your skills with such passion, determination, and inspiration.

CHAPTER 5:
Many "How-To's" to Land Your Next Position

- Learn that at each step of the interview process, there is an opportunity to leave them with a "WOW."
- Provide efficient and effective responses to interview questions; use the SAR approach to be clear and concise.
- After the initial interviews, giving a potential employer a 90-day plan for what you would do at his company will put you at the head of the line.

CHAPTER 6:
Your "Job," While Looking for a Job

- During your time in transition, be sure to schedule downtime from the hectic pace and stress of networking, interviewing, and job submission.
- "Transition life" itself is a flood of emotions and sometimes all in one day: Hope, depression, focus, fog, frustration, elation, second-guessing, pride, and on and on.
- Life moves fast, and if we stop learning and stop listening, we truly become lost.
- Even at your darkest times you can chose to lean forward and smile.
- Again, the basic concepts apply, but when you truly are interested in others, it will show, and those people will become your advisors and you can create followers that want to help you be more successful.

ABOUT THE AUTHOR

George's first book, *Hired: Cut Your Career Search Time in Half,* is based on his own experience—when he found himself facing two job transitions in less than three years. From both his military training and operations background, he learned that career transition also has a process. He became a student, listening, taking copious notes, and asking vital questions to many people that he met.

George started his career in the US Army serving in 101st Airborne Division in Fort Campbell, Kentucky, additionally in Wurzburg, Germany, and Kuwait, Saudi Arabia and Iraq in Support of Desert Shield/Desert Storm. He credits this experience with his leadership training, positive attitude through adversity, and his ability to overcome major obstacles. In addition, George has 25 years in Global Operations managing working in four industries: Automotive, Contract Electronic

Manufacturing, Industrial Automation, and Capital Equipment Manufacturing. He is passionate about helping individuals and businesses become better.

George has had three international assignments in Germany, Thailand and China, and these have increased his knowledge of global and diversified cultures.

He credits his strong belief in God and the support of his family for his success. His wife of 26 years, Kerry, is very loving and supportive, as are their three beautiful and successful children: Mason, Devin, and Aislynn. He loves spending his free time with his family boating, traveling, and golfing, plus he's an avid runner.

George also does individual coaching, consults with businesses and business leaders, as well as speaks on topics such as developing next generational leaders in organization, strong teams, driving improvements within companies.

To contact George for further assistance email him at:
georgecmurray@gmail.com.
Follow George on Instagram: @get_better_start_today
If this book helped connect with George on LinkedIn and let him know: https://www.linkedin.com/in/georgecmurray/